THE CH

& FLO

HANDBOOK

THE CHARTER & FLOTILLA HANDBOOK

Claire and Frank Wilson

fernhurst
BOOKS

First published in 1995 by Fernhurst Books, Duke's Path, High Street, Arundel, West Sussex, BN18 9AJ, UK

Printed and bound in Great Britain

British Library Cataloguing in Publication Data:
A catalogue record for this book is available from the British Library.

ISBN 1 898660-14-X

Acknowledgments
The authors and publisher would like to thank the Buckley family for the loan of their Jeanneau 28 *Equity* for the photo sessions, and Annie Buckley, Simon Davison, Bill Anderson, Peter Milne and the authors for crewing her.

Photographic credits
Cover photo courtesy of Sunsail
All other photos by Chris Davies or courtesy of the charter/flotilla companies Sunsail (The Port House, Port Solent, Portsmouth, Hampshire) and Templecraft and Odysseus (33 Grand Parade, Brighton, East Sussex)

Edited by Jeremy Evans
DTP by Creative Byte, Bournemouth
Cover design by Simon Balley
Printed and bound by Ebenezer Baylis & Son, Worcester
Text set in 8PT Rockwell Light

Contents

INTRODUCTION

Every year we answer questions at boat show stands. The most frequent is "How much experience do I need to be able to charter a yacht or join a flotilla?". Other questions are from those wanting to know what is available in the way of yachting holidays, and many are intrigued to know what a flotilla holiday is really all about. It was with these questions in mind that we realised the need to write this book.

From our experience of working as flotilla crew, and with independent as well as flotilla clients, we have seen the way in which these types of holidays allow people to discover the joys of warm weather sailing. Many come back year after year, some even chartering a yacht for the best part of a season in preference to owning their own. We have met people from many walks of life, with all manner of previous sailing experience, and with all sorts of needs when it comes to having a good holiday. We have experienced many of the problems that people come across when chartering. With this background, we have aimed to make this book as useful as possible to those new to chartering and to flotilla sailing. Have a great holiday!

Claire & Frank Wilson

PART ONE

WHAT IS A CHARTER?

1 Charter Choices

It is easy to see why places like Greece and Turkey are so popular for sailing holidays. Favourable climate, beautiful surroundings, safe cruising and a relaxed atmosphere make yacht charter and watersports holidays very attractive. Now Europeans are also enjoying visiting exotic places further afield, such as the Caribbean and the Pacific Ocean.

Charter yachts have changed considerably over the years. Light displacement yachts with a good performance are popular in places like the Mediterranean where charter is seasonal, restricted to when the weather is likely to be warm and predictable. Technological developments have meant yachts can be chosen that are much easier to handle and maintain. The roller furling genoa has done away with the need for a full wardrobe of sails and a crew large enough to handle them. VHF radio allows freedom to both flotilla and bareboat charterers, and other developments in communications and navigational equipment are making charter easier in many parts of the world. Changes to interiors have made yachts more comfortable. Spacious cabins and facilities such as fridges and showers are important to people on holiday in a warm climate, and consumer demand has meant they are usually found on most larger yachts and often on smaller ones as well.

Gaining sufficient experience to take a yacht bareboat, without skipper or crew, has not always been easy in the past. Nowadays far more opportunities exist for people to take up sailing, and with international travel so much easier yacht charter is no longer only for the very well off or those who have a yacht at home. In fact many recognise the benefit of not having their own yacht sitting idle for weeks on end, and prefer to spend their money on charters instead. The flotilla holiday is recognised for its part in introducing people to the joys of warm weather sailing, and has done much to encourage and develop the yacht charter business. Nowadays there are all manner of affordable sailing holidays, and the more common are outlined on the pages that follow in the first chapter.

Bareboat or independent charter

Bareboat charter is by no means as basic as it sounds. It simply means the hire of a yacht for a given length of time, rather like hiring a car. No skipper or crew are provided. Aspects of the charter such as the amount of support given by shore crew, how the yacht is fitted out and its type and condition will depend on the charter company involved.

Prices for bareboat charter are normally per yacht per week and exclusive of flights and transfers, though many companies can include travel arrangements as part of the deal. Other items such as fuel and mooring fees are also not normally included in the basic price. Yachts available for bareboat charter range from about 25 to 55 feet (7.5 to 17 metres) in length. Anything larger is unlikely to be on offer without a paid skipper.

Inland waterways

There are many inland waterways on which it is possible to charter a yacht, both motor and sail. Examples include the extensive canal system in France, the Norfolk Broads in England, and the West Highlands of Scotland. Motor yachts range from traditional narrow boats to modern cruisers, while gaff rigged sailing yachts may be found on the Norfolk Broads and modern sailing yachts on the lochs in Scotland.

Charter/purchase

Yachts are usually expensive to buy and to keep. Some companies offer the facility to co-purchase a new yacht. They charter and manage it for a few years, after which it becomes the property of the individual owner. Others invite people to buy a yacht from them, and then manage and charter it to pay expenses and give some income. In the meantime the yacht is also available for the owner or co-owners to use. Make sure you know where you stand if the company is not able to provide charters, and the boat is sitting idle.

Flotilla holidays

Chartering a yacht as part of a flotilla is not dissimilar from bareboat charter. The yacht is chartered without a skipper and crew, and with the responsibility that this entails. The difference is that it will be one of a group of yachts, commonly about ten, which is accompanied by a support crew (or lead crew) on board a separate yacht who act as guides, give help where needed, and decide which harbour or anchorage the flotilla will use at the end of each day. Part of the second half of the holiday will be allocated to free sailing where clients choose where they would like to go, and the flotilla then meets up again at the end of a few days.

Most flotillas are based in Greece and Turkey, though more recently others are becoming available in more far flung places such as the Caribbean and Thailand. Flotillas follow either a one or two week itinerary, and may be either a one way or return trip. Size of yachts varies between 25 and 43 feet (7.5 and 13 metres), and often all the yachts of a flotilla will be the same. Cost is normally an all-inclusive package with prices per person inclusive of flights and transfers, though it is possible to make your own travel arrangements as long as they fit in with the beginning and end of the flotilla. As with bareboat charter, the more people there are on the yacht, the cheaper it is per person.

An option for those wanting a little more independence is to take a flotilla yacht on bareboat charter. The flotilla support crew will be in the area should they be needed, and it may be possible to join in some of the social events as well. There may also be the option to join the flotilla for the first few days. Another possibility is for a group of bareboaters to arrange their own flotilla, perhaps with a local skipper as a guide.

Flotillas are popular with the British, Germans and Dutch. Most will be predominantly of one nationality, but some are advertised in more than one country and are therefore mixed.

Combined holidays

Numerous options exist for those not wanting to spend their entire holiday on board a yacht. Some companies offer alternatives such as villa-flotilla, stay-and-sail and club holidays. A holiday combining a week ashore preceded or followed by a week or two on flotilla or bareboat charter is a popular option. Frequently there will be other watersports on offer during the week ashore, such as windsurfing and dinghy sailing. Some of these holidays offer the option of learning to sail a

Docking at the end of another wonderful day on the water. That is what chartering is all about!

yacht during the week ashore followed by a week on flotilla, and are therefore open to novice sailors.

Other packages now available include the option to day-sail a yacht as part of a shore-based holiday; activities for children; learning to sail; or a few days on board a luxury skippered yacht. Whatever your preference, there will be a holiday to suit, and some companies will tailor-make holidays to individual needs.

Skippered and crewed charter

There are two kinds of skippered charter. The first is similar in many ways to bareboat charter, with a skipper and/or crew taken on as extras. You can have a skipper if you lack the experience to go completely bareboat, or an extra pair of hands to help with sailing if you have a young family on board, or someone to do the cooking. Prices are the same as bareboat, with a daily supplement for skipper and/or crew. They will require a separate cabin, and you will often be expected to pay for their meals on board. There may also be the option to have a skipper come with you for the first few days until you get used to a new yacht or area.

The second type of charter is where a yacht is

Some charter companies offer the option of combining a shore-based holiday with a flotilla, giving a combination of cruiser sailing, dinghy sailing and windsurfing.

managed by a permanent skipper or skipper and crew, and clients join them as guests. Just what is included will depend on local facilities and attractions, size of yacht and number of crew required, price of charter, and whether the skipper and crew are employed or own the yacht themselves. Some charters will provide all meals on board, and others only those during the day. Some offer other activities such as windsurfing, scuba diving, big game fishing, waterskiing and shore excursions. Company managed charters may offer some of these services as standard, along with cordon bleu cookery.

Owner skippers and crew provide services as abilities and resources permit, so that no two will be the same. All manner of features may be available such as TV and video, CD player, use of camcorder or underwater camera, fishing equipment, air conditioning, freezer, communication systems and sophisticated electronic navigational equipment. Not all of these features are exclusive to crewed charters, but many require power supplies, maintenance and operational skills that make them only practical on a yacht with permanent crew. The spectrum is immense. Yachts on offer range from smallish 40 footers to the very large, up to 200 feet (60 metres) or more. They may be the very latest design, restored classics, or traditional wooden yachts such as a Gulet in Turkey. They may be anything from cruiser to out-

and-out racer, from fairly simple to luxurious, with every available gadget and comfort above and below decks. There are motor yachts, sailing yachts and those that do a bit of both. You can have one crew for every three guests or three to every one, and you can take the whole thing or share it with others. They can be extremely expensive or fairly reasonable. All in all there is plenty to choose from!

Multihulls

Multihulled yachts (catamarans and trimarans) are available on both bareboat and crewed charter. They are popular with those wanting spacious living accomodation and a yacht that does not tilt when sailing. Their shallow draft makes them useful for snorkelling or diving on coral reefs, and there are often options on crewed charters in areas such as the Caribbean.

Motor yachts

Motor yachts are available for charter in much the same way as sailing yachts, but are more likely to have crew and be towards the more expensive end of the market. Prices tend to be quite a bit higher than for sailing yachts of an equivalent size, whether crewed or bareboat. Due to past restrictions, motor yachts are rarely available for bareboat charter in Greece. At the time of writing we know of a motor yacht flotilla in

Turkey for which no experience is required.

When a yacht is advertised as being a motor-sailer, it will be somewhere between the two, usually with a larger engine and lower sailing performance than a sailing yacht of similar size. The engine on a sailing yacht is known as an auxiliary engine as it is not the primary source of power.

Adventure charter

Adventure charters include ecological trips studying marine life such as whales, dolphins and coral; ocean voyages or coastal trips on a 19th century Brigantine; voyages to remote parts of the world; and the opportunity to experience sailing on a performance yacht that has previously completed a round the world race. Trips can be as short as a few days to as long as several weeks.

Racing charter

Some opportunities exist for chartering a yacht for racing, such as entering a programme of races in the Caribbean. Security deposits are considerably higher to cover the increased cost of insurance for racing, as the risks of yacht damage are that much greater.

Corporate charter

Corporate charter is where a yacht is chartered by a group of individuals such as business associates for a day out, entertainment, or a character-building exercise. A number of companies now offer this form of charter.

Yacht share options

Yacht charter is by no means restricted to those having friends, family or a partner with whom to share a sailing holiday. A number of companies cater for those not able or wishing to make up a complete crew by offering yacht share options. Couples as well as singles can opt to share a yacht for reasons such as financial considerations, lack of sailing experience, or wanting to meet people.

One way to find potential yacht sharers is to advertise in the yachting or local press. Alternatively some companies offer a facility which puts people in touch with other enquirers to enable them to get a crew together themselves. If you can cope with taking pot luck, some companies will put crews together. Sailing experience is taken into consideration when deciding who goes with whom, making it a possible option for novice or inexperienced sailors. Yacht share is frequently restricted to certain dates in order to produce a group that is more likely to mix well. It is

A big multihull is a popular choice for charter in the Caribbean. It offers a great deal of deck space, and unlike a conventional monohull, cannot heel over. The main disadvantages are that multihulls are expensive, and take up more space in marinas.

also sometimes available on combined shore-based and flotilla holidays where crews meet each other in the first week, and some skippered charters also organise yacht sharing. There can be quite a variation in size of yacht and numbers per yacht on offer, so it is worth checking out all the available options.

Delivery cruises

It is a strange thing that while some people make a living being paid to move boats from place to place, others pay for the privilege. Companies needing to move fleets of boats – maybe at the end of a season or when a new fleet is delivered – will find crews by offering reduced-price delivery trips to more experienced sailors. A lead crew will also be there to organise the trip. Disadvantages are that trips will normally be out of season when weather conditions may not be good, and there is the pressure of a time limit. A brand new boat may also seem attractive, but there may be problems on a maiden voyage.

2 Life On Charter

The flotilla briefing usually takes place every morning. A convivial location such as a local café makes it an occasion which can sensibly be combined with breakfast.

WHAT TO EXPECT
Briefings

There are three aspects to the information and advice you should be given before setting off, whether on bareboat charter or flotilla. These are the yacht, boat handling and mooring, and the cruising area. It is only possible to give guidelines about what to expect.

The yacht. When being given a briefing on the yacht, you should be shown where everything is, above and below decks, and how it works. Below decks this may include safety equipment, operation of the VHF radio, the electrics, the fridge, the cooker, the toilet, the bilge pumps, the fresh water system and where to fill the water tank, the engine and daily checks, and the

seacocks. Above decks this may include more safety equipment, the anchors, the standing and running rigging, the sails and any roller furling systems, the dinghy or tender, and how to operate the engine.

This is the time to ask if you are not sure how anything works. You will probably also be advised on things to avoid, such as flattening the batteries or jamming the roller furling system. This briefing should include everyone on board.

Boat handling and mooring. It is helpful to have a practical demonstration of the handling characteristics of the yacht, as well as the types of mooring found in the area. On flotilla this is often done as a group, with the flotilla skipper taking representatives from each

One of the first things you should do is check through the inventory. Make sure you have got what you need, and that nothing has been lost or over-looked from the previous charterers.

boat onto one of the yachts, and running through things such as how to set and reef the sails, how to handle the yacht under engine, and how to moor. In the Mediterranean they would probably carry out a bows-to mooring, and perhaps cover anchoring as well. The first chance skippers will have to practice these manoeuvres will be when they set out on the first day. Not all charterers will receive practical demonstrations, though information may be passed on verbally.

The cruising area. Most companies want their clients to remain within a specified cruising area and to be aware of local hazards such as unmarked shoals and reefs. Some will ask that boats remain in harbour in adverse weather conditions, or when the forecast is bad. Many will also give advice about good places to moor, where to obtain supplies, and who to call in the event of problems. If information is brief, it can help to have a list of questions to ask.

On flotilla, the briefing is given daily to a group. Daily briefings mean that much more information can be given which is specific to that day, such as navigation involved, places of interest and good restaurants. The briefing will often take place outside a local café, so breakfast or coffee can be enjoyed at the same time. It will rarely take place before nine in the morning!

Inventory checks

Clients should be given a written list of items on board under headings such as galley, safety and navigational equipment, bedding, winch and bilge pump handles, dinghy and oars, fenders, anchors and mooring lines. There will be enough crockery and cutlery for each person, and safety equipment such as life jackets will be sufficient to meet regulations so there may be more than you need. The company staff will have aimed to check the inventory before you arrive, but checking the list yourself will help you know what there is and where it is situated, as well as highlighting anything missing.

At the end of the charter you will usually be expected to complete the inventory check again and write down anything that was lost, broken or damaged. Some companies want to check the yacht over themselves, others rely on the charterers' word. It is worth pointing out to company staff if anything is obviously faulty or damaged at the start of the holiday, so that it can be rectified if possible and in case there will be a problem later deciding if you were responsible. Staff also find it helpful if any faults are

Sailing off into the blue yonder is all very fine, but there are rules and regulations wherever you go. The local authorities may insist on specific papers, and you should be able to provide these with no problem.

pointed out at the end of the charter, in order to make repairs in the limited time available before the next clients arrive. If you have a complaint about something, the time to report it is before you leave, even if it will be dealt with later.

Security deposits and insurance

Although yachts are insured against damage or loss, the first part of any claim, the excess, is not paid by the insurers. This sum is covered either by paying a security deposit at the start of the holiday, or insurance to cover this amount. Some companies will offer the option to choose one or the other, but there

may be no choice.

In the case of the security deposit, it is refunded if the yacht is returned without loss or damage. Some items such as a fender should not cost you dear, but larger items such as a dinghy or outboard motor or structural damage to the yacht could cost a lot to replace or repair. It is not possible to make claims for company property on personal holiday insurance, as you would for your own. Some deposits are large which should not be overlooked when considering the price of the holiday. Security insurance on the other hand is usually a minor sum in comparison, but of course is non-refundable.

With some policies there may still be a few items

such as binoculars that must be paid for if lost. As with all insurance, it is much easier to decide if it was worth it in retrospect. Occasionally a company will ask for a fidelity deposit to cover items such as fuel, if for example a yacht is not returned with a full tank as agreed.

It is often possible to pay security insurance at the time of booking. If you have to pay a security deposit on arrival, you need to check the method of payment in advance. They may ask for local currency or Eurocheques. Due to restrictions on the amount you are allowed to put on one cheque, you may be asked for several. In places such as Greece and Turkey, cheques are normally kept and returned unused due to the administrative difficulties which are involved in banking them and reimbursing the client. Companies will not necessarily refund the deposit at the time the yacht is returned, but should agree beforehand to do so within a certain number of days.

Boat papers

Charter yachts will often carry a set of papers, including items such as registration documents, certificates of compliance with safety regulations, insurance documents, VHF radio licence, and crew lists. If sailing licences are required, it is a good idea to keep them with the papers in case they need to be seen by port authorities. A yacht may not legally be able to go anywhere without these papers, so leave them somewhere appropriate such as in the chart table.

What to ask

Often yachts will remain at the charter base until the day after the clients arrive, due to the time it takes to get everything done. On a bareboat charter it will be necessary to find out certain things before setting out, and some companies will send out copies of cruising notes at the time of booking to help people prepare. There are also many Pilot Guides available for those wanting to do some advance research into the area.

1. *What to do in the event of problems - who to call and how?*
Find out how to contact the company base, who to contact in emergency and which local services such as engineers or doctors should be used. Find out what to do in the event of loss or theft, and when the company will need to know about damage or other problems.

2. *VHF channels for other information.*

You may need to know about weather forecasts or restaurants, which VHF channels to use for ship-to-ship, and which to avoid. Ask for a radio check before you leave.

3. *How and where to make phone calls.*
Internationally, shore-to-shore, or ship-to-shore if facilities exist.

4. *Money changing.*
Where is best? Bureaux or banks?

5. *Formalities.*
Port authorities - anything you must do to comply with local laws.

6. *Specific instructions for the yacht.*
Such as engine checks and how to bleed the engine.

7. *Local information.*
Good harbours and anchorages, where to get water and fuel if required, help needed in interpreting the charts.

8. *Local weather information.*
What to expect and when not to go.

9. *Local hazards.*
Flora and fauna, unsafe drinking water, snakes, theft.

CREATURE COMFORTS

Whether or not you enjoy living on a yacht has a lot to do with the type of person you are, your expectations, the yacht itself and where it is based. To some people exhilarating sailing makes anything worthwhile; to others being wet, cold and thrown about is a turn-off, and if combined with uncomfortable living conditions they will not come back for more.

Unless you are very unlucky, most charter yachts provide at least a fair degree of comfort, and at best can be downright luxurious. Life on board is never going to be the same as at home, and to many this is much of the attraction. Sailing holidays in warm climates lend themselves to a relaxed way of life that tends to make things such as washing-up and creature comforts seem less important. Of course, if you are planning a trip on the Norfolk Broads in February you may need to work a bit harder on your state of mind!

Electrical appliances

Whether you decide to take electrical appliances such as shavers and hair driers will depend on whether

A warm climate encourages non-stop alfresco eating. Many charterers opt to make the most of the cockpit table and eat breakfast and lunch on board, and then explore the local restaurants each evening.

there will be the facility to plug them in. Larger yachts may well be able to provide 110 or 220 volts via a generator or invertor, but many will only have access to 12 or possibly 24 volts.

Shore power is only going to be available in 'developed' places such as marinas. If it is likely to be available you will also need to check the voltage. Northern Europe, France, Italy, Greece and Turkey all use 220/240 volts. In the Caribbean it varies between 110 and 240 volts throughout the islands. Some local restaurants will allow you to plug a battery charger into their supply.

Many items such as camcorder battery chargers, rechargeable shavers and even hand-held GPS units can be used from a 12 volt supply. Not all yachts will have the facility to plug into it, and if there is a socket it may be of the cigarette lighter type found in cars. Alternatively, it may be a small socket for which a suitable plug can be provided, in which case the polarity of the terminals should be checked to make sure the appliance is not damaged by connecting the poles the wrong way. Adaptors for items requiring a lower voltage should be taken as well. The charter company should be able to tell you what will be available.

Self-catering

Just how much self-catering you need to do and how easy it will be to get hold of supplies will depend on where you go, and whether you have a cook to shop for you. Throughout much of the Mediterranean provisioning and eating out are fairly easy, even though you may not have much choice. Storage of food is not a problem if you can buy supplies when you need them, and even in smaller villages in Greece the local shop is usually able to supply most basic provisions, though prices may be higher than at home. Parts of the Turkish coast are more isolated and provisions harder to come by, so that stocking up well when you can is generally a good idea. The town of Marmaris, for example, where many bareboat charters and some flotillas are based, is a good place for supplies. Turkey often has excellent markets, as do Italy and France.

Eating out in France, Corsica and Italy is generally more expensive than Greece and Turkey, though differences are becoming less. Wine and locally produced spirits are often inexpensive in the Mediterranean, even in Turkey where the Moslem culture might be expected not to encourage alcohol.

When chartering in other parts of the world such

as the Caribbean or Pacific there may be fewer facilities for provisioning and eating out and you may expect to eat a certain number of meals on board. Charter companies in these areas will often offer a range of provisioning services. In some parts of the Caribbean shopping is becoming much easier with local shops catering for the needs of charterers, but you may have the option to have some or all supplies already provided. Many yachts, both in the Mediterranean and elsewhere, come with a starter pack of basic supplies such as cleaning materials and beverages, and foods that range from basic to fairly comprehensive.

Many nationalities have tastes in food that are peculiar to themselves. Even in areas that are used to catering for tourists you may not be able to get hold of all items you require, so if there is something you cannot do without you may want to take it with you. English tea-bags (larger and stronger than many other varieties) and Marmite are two examples. Vegetarians may not always find themselves well catered for. If you want to go out every evening, you may have to make sure you get what you need in the way of food at other times of the day. If you eat fish, be warned that in the Mediterranean it can be very expensive. Prices are often worked out according to weight.

Water

Check if it is sensible to drink the local water. Visitors to Turkey are sometimes affected by stomach upsets, and drinking only bottled or boiled water may be advisable. Many people prefer not to drink water directly from the tanks on board, unless it is filtered. Even if the tanks are regularly cleaned and emptied, you cannot be sure that someone has not filled them up from a suspect supply, so drinking bottled water is often advised with tank water only drunk if boiled.

Personal functions

Lack of privacy and space may not concern you if you are sailing with the family. If sharing a yacht with friends or people you have never met before, this may be more important. Noises from the toilet or snoring are not easily contained, and can be embarrassing if you are the sensitive type. It is just the same for everyone, so if you do not think you will be able to sleep at night you can take earplugs.

Shore facilities such as toilets and showers are usually available in marinas. Elsewhere they are often provided by restaurants and hotels. Solar showers can be extremely efficient at heating water, so much so that it may be necessary to make sure they are not too

hot. Normally they are left clear side up. If the water is too hot, try turning them around the other way with the reflective side at the top. On board you will often need to be careful about how you use your fresh water supply. Water tanks are not always that large, and it is not always possible to fill up as often as you would like.

Clothing

A common mistake made by holiday charterers is to take far too much luggage. Some places will of course demand warm clothes and full wet weather gear, but many destinations do not and smart clothes are only needed if you want to sample the night life. Shorts, t-shirts and swimwear are commonly worn during the day, and shirts, light trousers or skirts in the evenings. Take some clothes which cover you completely to ward off insects and sunburn.

Rubber soled shoes are good on deck, and an old pair of shoes for swimming can protect against sea urchins and coral. An old pair of gardening gloves for handling the anchor and chain will be cheaper than buying a special sailing pair. A light waterproof jacket is always a good idea, because even if it does not rain there can still be sea spray. Unless it is likely to be cold you may not want to bother with leggings, as bare legs do not take long to dry.

Washing clothes will probably not be high on your list of priorities. Laundry facilities may sometimes be available, but whether you are able to do it yourself in a launderette or have to hand over the items will depend on where you are. If it is the latter, they may ask you to come back next day which may be of no use. Washing things through and drying them on a line (often provided) or the safety rails may be simpler, and is not as frowned on as at home.

Bags

Soft, collapsible bags are much easier to manage on a yacht than suitcases. You may have a hanging locker for clothes that need a little more care, though other stowage may be limited. Another good reason not to take too much gear is if you plan to fill every available bunk, when copious amounts of luggage can leave you tripping over yourselves.

Sunburn and sun

Sunburn can take you unawares. Not only are the sun's rays potentially more damaging in many hot parts of the world, but reflected rays off the sea and white sails can make exposure much higher. When there is a breeze and you are otherwise occupied,

Beware the sun. A cooling breeze and the sea tickling your feet means you do not realise how hot it really is. The risk of sunburn should be taken seriously, as should dehydration – so keep drinking!

you may not be aware of what is happening.

A good pair of sunglasses is essential to protect against glare from the sun, and a hat or visor will help keep it off the face and head. High protection waterproof sunblocks will protect those parts of the body particularly at risk such as noses, tops of ears, tops of the feet and the back when snorkelling. Taking it slowly when getting a tan is much better than frying on the first day, besides which it gives you wrinkles!

You will probably feel much better in the sun for drinking plenty of fluids, and not the alcoholic kind which can have the opposite effect, even from the evening before. It is quite easy to get dehydrated, and it is surprising how much you need to drink to counter ill effects such as headaches.

Pests

Some cruising areas such as Thailand are known to have a malarial risk, but although the mosquito is common in many areas of the Mediterranean and Caribbean, its presence is mostly only irritating as opposed to dangerous. Parts of North Africa, Turkey, Haiti and the Dominican Republic carry some risk. The sand fly comes out at night in places such as the Caribbean and causes a nasty itch similar to the mosquito. They are extremely small and will attack unnoticed, often earning the name *noseeums*.

You will probably want to avoid being woken up in the night by a buzzing in the ear and a mosquito that eludes you whenever you turn the light on. Wearing a sheet and some form of repellent will help, especially if you are the type they seem to like. Some people take pieces of netting to rig over open hatches to help keep them out, and mosquito nets designed for use over a bunk can also be effective though you will probably not want to invest in one unless you know there will be a problem. Mosquito coils that burn to produce a rather unattractive smoke (do not leave one lit in an unventilated cabin) and citronella candles can be useful in the open air. Gadgets that vaporise a tablet or liquid may also be of use if you can get one that runs off your electrical supply.

Mosquitos have a habit of lurking on board until the evening, when they will come out and find you. If this is a big problem and you are going out, you could try spraying the boat with insect killer before shutting it up. Make sure it is well ventilated before you go back down below. If you are anchored away from the shore and there is a breeze they may well not be able to find you.

During the day flies and wasps would often rather share your lunch than find their own, so do not leave food or crumbs about and get rid of all rubbish.

How many?

When company literature gives the number of berths available on a bareboat or flotilla yacht it is usually referring to the maximum number possible, and will therefore normally include bunks in the saloon as well as in cabins. Price may decide whether or not you wish to fill every berth, but if your concern is for comfort take less than the maximum.

A forepeak cabin may be fine for a couple, but a little claustrophobic and lacking in leg room for singles. In some forward cabins the bunks will be moveable to accommodate crew as you wish. A saloon bunk may convert to a double, but only a small one. If there is a quarter berth such as on a smaller yacht, it may be a narrow bunk open to the saloon into which the occupant has to crawl feet first. Some brochures will advise as to berth lengths and widths. In general if all the crew have a berth in a cabin, the accommodation will be comfortable.

Cool air

Encouraging air to circulate below decks may simply be a matter of opening hatches if there is a good breeze. Yachts in northern waters tend to have forepeak hatches that open towards the stern to help keep spray out. On yachts in warmer climates they open towards the bow to help air flow in, and a device known as a windscoop rigged up through the hatch helps further. Sun awnings and bimini tops are a means of keeping the sun off the cockpit, which is frequently a necessity in hot climates. Bimini tops have a semi-permanent rigid frame, but sun awnings usually drape over the boom and are not intended for use when sailing.

Hot air

Heating is not normally available on the average charter yacht designed for warm weather cruising, even if parts of the season can be a little cooler. Air conditioning will normally seem more appropriate, but both this and heating are usually only found on larger vessels such as motor yachts, or perhaps on a privately owned yacht or on more expensive charters with an emphasis on comfort. Yachts chartered in cooler climates may well have heating. Diesel-powered warm air heating is popular, as it does not add to the problems of condensation or battery power consumption.

Small items

Clanking halyards, squeaking fenders and snatching shore lines are some of the things that make it difficult to sleep at night. Tie back halyards away from the mast, try a squirt of washing-up liquid on noisy fenders, and loosen off lines to the shore to give more slack and less jerks.

Anything dropped over the side rarely floats, and unless you are lucky enough to be in clear shallow water will not be seen again. Sunglasses, shoes, wallets and cameras are particularly at risk. Glasses can be secured with a string around the neck, and cameras should always be used with a neck strap. Shoes often float long enough to grab them with a boathook if you are quick.

The cost of cleaning at the end of the holiday may or may not be included in the price of a bareboat or flotilla yacht. Frequently you are expected to leave it as you found it, with the option to have someone else clean it for you at a price. Bed linen is usually provided, though towels may not be. Such details are usually specified in the company literature.

LOCAL ETIQUETTE
Environment

It is unfortunate that yacht charter can cause sea pollution and damage to local flora and fauna. Knowing how to avoid these problems will benefit both the environment and yourselves, as some authorities take a very dim view of those flouting regulations and have substantial fines to match.

Do not add to the litter problem by throwing it over the side, even if everyone else seems to. Rubbish disposal services vary from place to place, and it may mean carrying it with you to the next major port of call. Just because there is a pile of rubbish on the shore does not mean it is a recognised site. Leaving one bag of rubbish can lead someone else to do the same, and before you know it there is a sizeable pile left to fester for months in the sun. If you do need to carry rubbish for more than a day, throw perishable food-stuffs over the side and wash out tins and containers to discourage insects and bad smells. Plastic is a particular problem, and will never degrade if you chuck it overboard.

The aim of fitting a holding tank to a marine toilet is to avoid discharging waste into harbours and

Always respect the local environment. The local people were there before you and will remain there when you go away. It is important that you make your visit enjoyable for them as well as for yourselves.

anchorages, and in some countries into the sea altogether. In many inland waterways waste must be disposed of at pumping-out stations, and in some areas such as Turkey discharging waste into the sea near to the shore may be met by stiff fines. If the tank is not emptied regularly you risk allowing it to overflow, which is unpleasant as well as a risk to health, especially if anyone is swimming or a dinghy is floating nearby.

Diesel spillage is always to be avoided, and there is no hiding a spill because even a little goes an awful long way. Port authorities may take it even more seriously than sewage. To prevent overflowing, pour the diesel in slowly and do not fill the funnel too full. Watch that none spills out of the tank overflow. A squirt of detergent such as washing-up liquid will help disperse spills, but not the pollution they cause.

Fishing

Many people like to do a bit of fishing on holiday. Check first that fishing is allowed, whether you need a permit, or if there is anything that must not be caught. Female lobsters for example are protected in many parts of the Caribbean, and spearfishing is prohibited in many cruising areas.

Coral

Coral reefs are one of the attractions of visiting tropical waters such as the Caribbean and Pacific. Despite the damage they can do to the hull of a boat, the living surface is delicate and easily damaged, and pieces of coral can easily be broken off when diving or anchoring. Taking coral may be prohibited, and buying souvenirs should be avoided. Yachts at anchor are believed to present a considerable risk to reefs, so be careful to avoid dropping the anchor on coral. Clear waters mean that reefs are easily seen, and a hand on the line can help to feel if an anchor is on coral as opposed to sand.

Treasures

Turkey is well known for its historical remains, some of which lie beneath the sea. The taking of artifacts such as amphorae is prohibited, as it is in other countries such as Greece.

Water

Copious supplies of fresh water are not always available in warm climates such as Greece. Don't waste water by using it to wash the decks unless it is understood to be OK to do so. Water can be an expensive commodity which is saved from one winter to the next.

Fires

Barbecues are popular on warm evenings. Yachts in the Caribbean are frequently provided with a stainless steel barbecue that can be attached to the stern rail so that cooking is done on board. Do not light fires on the beach unless you know it is permitted. Many areas such as parts of the Mediterranean are prone to devastation by fires, and lighting them is often prohibited. Very few spots may be available to flotillas for barbecues, and they have to take great care not to cause damage that would jeopardise them in the future.

Clothes off

Despite the fact that many people enjoy the privacy of a yacht to expose more surface area to the sun than perhaps they normally would, nudity is not necessarily accepted in the country being visited and in some is illegal.

Be careful not to cause offence or break any laws by dressing in a way unacceptable to local people, whether it be in town or on the beach.

Drugs

Being found in possession of drugs, let alone being found using or selling them, is a serious offence in the Mediterranean, Caribbean and many other parts of the world. Penalties can include confiscation of the yacht and imprisonment as well as fines, even for the more innocuous varieties. Yachts in the Caribbean and Bahamas can be stopped and searched by the coastguard without warning.

MONEY & COMMUNICATIONS

Find out before you go which type and form of currency it is advisable to have. Check if you need any money to pay for items such as security deposits and cruising permits, and if so in which form. It is always an idea to take a certain amount of local currency, because the nature of such holidays is that you may not have the opportunity to change money for a few days, especially if you arrive at a weekend.

Even though a bank may tell you that regular banking facilities are good in the country concerned, they may be few and far between in those parts you will be visiting, especially if you do not go near any larger towns. Your charter company or booking agent should be able to give advice. If you are desperate for money when on charter, banks will often arrange money transfers to a local bank but may charge a high price for the service.

Credit cards

Credit cards may not be widely accepted in the areas you are visiting, even if they are in more developed parts of the country. This is the case in Greece and Turkey for example, though you may be able to obtain money with a credit card at a bank if you can find one. Using a credit card in a bank in Italy can take at least an hour, and a lot of patience. Even in the Caribbean, where credit cards are fairly widely used, they may not be taken in smaller restaurants.

Travellers cheques

Travellers cheques are widely accepted. Find out which currency to take, and have some smaller denominations for use in restaurants and shops.

Eurocheques

Eurocheques are widely accepted in many parts of Europe, though not all, and also in some places further afield. In Turkey it will be possible to cash a cheque in a bank, but not in retail outlets such as shops and hotels. Cheques are normally written in local currency, and the rate worked out by the bank at home. Banks usually have a yearly charge for issuing Eurocheques and a Eurocheque card. One advantage is that there is no decision to be made beforehand as to how much currency to take. Just as with a credit card, some banks will have the facility for a Eurocheque card to be used in their automatic cash dispensers.

Variable currencies

Currency may vary from island to island. In the Windward Islands, for example, the French franc is used in Martinique and the rest use the Eastern Caribbean dollar, with the US dollar often acceptable as well.

Postal services

Some postal services are not good, and if the only post boxes you come across are on small islands it could be a while before the postman comes and empties them. If you want to be sure a message will get back quickly, it may be better to send a fax. Many tourist offices offer a fax service. If you need to have mail sent out to you, you may be able to arrange to receive a fax and marinas will usually hold mail.

The postal service available in many countries, where post labelled *Post Restante* can be sent to a main post office and collected, is only going to be useful if you know exactly where it will go and that you will be able to collect it. It may be better to have it sent to the charter company base.

Some crewed charter yachts have all manner of electronic wizardry on board, enabling you to stay in touch with the office and business associates wherever you are in the world. Is that what you want?

Telephones

Telephone systems vary. Public phones in France and Italy are very good, using either coins or a phonecard. The Turkish system also uses phonecards that are widely available. The Greek phone system varies from place to place, made more difficult by the numerous small islands. Sometimes perseverance is required before being able to get through. Satellite services are bringing improvements, and payment is usually easy with calls being metered and charged by the unit. As well as the phone office or OTE, phones can be easily be found in tourist offices and street-side kiosks. Phonecards have also recently been introduced in Greece. Phone systems vary throughout the Caribbean, some using telephone credit cards, and others being less sophisticated.

To make a direct dialled international call:
1. Dial the international code to get outside the country.
2. Dial the code for the country you are calling.
3. Dial the phone number, but omit the zero from the beginning of the area code.

VHF and other communications

Developments in communications rarely stand still for very long. Very high frequency radio (VHF) has been in use for many years, and is almost universal where yachts are concerned. Marine VHF uses a certain range of frequencies and a set number of channels, each allocated a certain use such as inter-ship or port operations, depending on the country concerned. Channel 16 is used internationally as the distress and calling channel, and is monitored by such services as the coastguard and coast radio stations, as well as all commercial vessels. VHF radio provides communication over a relatively short range, and is frequently all that is needed.

Sometimes the VHF radio can be used to connect into the national telephone system, via a coast radio station. Some countries are better at this than others. In the British Virgin Islands for example, Radio Tortola will be able to connect you and other services such as a hospital or charter base, as well as inform you of incoming calls known as 'traffic'. In places like Greece, getting in touch with a coast station will not be as easy, and cannot be relied on as a means of communication.

If you hope to use this form of communication it is advisable to find out if it is available beforehand, and if so make prior arrangements with regards to payment such as by credit card, or with charges made to a home account.

Other radio frequencies are also used in marine

communications. The Navtex service uses a medium frequency to broadcast weather and navigational information via transmitters at coastal radio stations. The coverage throughout much of Europe is very good, and as systems are relatively cheap they are increasingly being used by yachts.

For vessels needing to communicate over a range greater than about 30 miles (48 kilometres), medium (MF) and high frequency (HF) radio waves may be used. Marine radios making use of these wave bands use what is known as a single side band (SSB). Some just use MF and some use both MF and HF. MF give a possible range of up to 300 miles (480 kilometres), and HF up to several thousand, with an international distress frequency and access to telephone networks via coast radio stations. Other information such as weather facsimile broadcasts is available with the appropriate equipment via an SSB radio. Operation of this type of radio requires skill and licensing, and calls connected to the telephone network will have to be paid for. SSB radios are therefore unlikely to be found on anything but crewed yachts.

A newer service known as autolink is now available for use with MF, HF or VHF radios, and allows direct dialling ship-to-shore via a coast radio station in countries where the necessary equipment is installed. This is only likely to be available on a bareboat charter if the charter company is able to ensure payment is made for calls.

Mobile phones

Cellular telephones are widely used throughout the Caribbean and Bahamas, with many bareboat yachts being provided with them. The phone company issues a number and arranges how you will pay, such as by credit card, and will also rent out phones if one is not provided. It may not be possible to use your own phone, as some UK and USA systems are incompatible. Use in other parts of the world will vary as to where you are; check, register with that country, and get issued with a number before you go.

Satcom

Satellite communication systems (Satcom) are becoming increasingly common on yachts as systems originally designed for larger vessels are adapted for their use. Cost of equipment and usage is still fairly high, and again they are only likely to be found on crewed charters, and usually the more expensive ones. Those available to smaller vessels are Inmarsat M and Inmarsat C. Inmarsat M allows voice and fax communications, and more recently a

data transfer service, and allows automatic direct dialling to many countries. Inmarsat C is what is known as a digital store-and-forward messaging service that allows messages to be transmitted and received worldwide, either via the telephone network to a computer terminal or fax, or via the telex network.

As part of the Global Maritime Distress and Safety System (GMDSS), Inmarsat satellites may be used via this system to send distress calls, and to track the newer emergency position indicating radio beacons (EPIRBs). Small personal varieties of these beacons may be worn on a lifejacket, and indicate their direction via a receiver should the wearer fall overboard.

CHILDREN ON CHARTER

Here are some of the things we think are important where children on sailing holidays are concerned.

Climate

There are many advantages to taking children sailing somewhere warm; they don't have to wear many clothes, they can swim every day, and they can snorkel, fish and mess about in the dinghy which in turn makes it easier on you. Washing on deck is easy with a solar shower, and clothes can be washed through and dried in no time.

School holidays may prevent you from avoiding the hottest times of year. Young skin is particularly susceptible to sunburn, and children are less able to cope with overheating, especially the very young. High protection waterproof sun creams, sunhats, loose cotton clothes, cool showers, and plenty of fluids to drink will help. In the Mediterranean you usually find local people taking a siesta in the heat of the day and making the most of the relative cool of the evening. It is not uncommon to see children out to all hours of the evening with their families. Encouraging your children to have a sleep in the day is a good idea if you spend most evenings ashore.

Mosquitos can make life miserable, so take plenty of insect repellent and itch relievers, and cover up at dusk and at night. You may be able to rig up a mosquito net over a child's bunk.

Warm weather holiday destinations are not always warm. In the Mediterranean for example it can still be wet and cool at the beginning and end of the sailing season. Bareboat and flotilla yachts rarely have heating, so condensation and damp may be a problem which you will have to consider, especially for very young children.

Children can have a great time on a flotilla, particularly if there are other children of the same age. They need their freedom and their own social set to make the most of it rather than just drag along with their parents.

Cruising area and choice of yacht

Some areas may be more suited to family cruising than others. You may want to avoid long trips or demanding sailing, and allow time for lunch stops and days off, especially on a two week holiday. Many modern charter yachts are ideal for families, having swim ladders on a wide stern to make getting on and off into the water or dinghy easier, as well as spacious interiors and plenty of bunks. If you think you will be shorthanded under way with one adult looking after a young child, you may want to choose a yacht that is designed for ease of handling, with sails that can be reefed or furled from the cockpit or an autopilot.

Food

Parents usually have a good idea what their children will not eat. If you are self-catering many places will sell familiar tinned foods, and dry goods such as rice or pasta are fairly universal. It may be worth stocking up with things you know you can use when you have the chance. If you eat out in the evenings, some places are used to catering for tourists with less adventurous tastes, and provide items such as pizzas and the inevitable chip. If you get tired of your children living

on chips and ice cream, or if they get fractious waiting for food while you enjoy a pre-dinner drink or the service is not as swift as you would like, it may be an idea to give them their meal before you go. On a crewed charter your cook will want to know about special requirements, such as for children or vegetarians.

Safety

When it is hot and sunny the last thing many children want to do is wear a lifejacket or harness, but you really need to decide beforehand at which point you will have to insist they do. Even if the water is warm, it can still be difficult to stay afloat if the sea is at all rough. Recovering a child lost overboard is rarely quick and easy, and if the water is cold they will be less able to cope with it than an adult. Some children are strong swimmers but it is always a shock falling in and it is probably true to say that the younger they are the more care you will need to take.

With some children you will need to be just as vigilant when on the quay as underway, but in the end only you can decide when and where lifejackets or harnesses need to be worn. Think about the times when falling overboard is most likely to occur, such as

The easy ages for children on yachts are the very young who cannot even crawl, and those who are old enough to swim with confidence. In between children may be a worry, but it is very much a case of the parents' attitude.

when walking about on deck, when underway or climbing into the dinghy, and if in doubt play safe.

Some companies will provide lifejackets for young children, but unless you are absolutely sure they will fit it is advisable to take your own. It is important they fit correctly, as too big is as bad as too small (usually measured in terms of weight). If you plan to take a lifejacket with an automatic inflation device, check that the airline is prepared to let you fly with it. Such items normally need to be carried as hand luggage. Unlike a lifejacket, a buoyancy aid will not give total support in the water, but is often less bulky to wear.

Children's harnesses should be adjustable. If you can't find one small enough you may need to adapt one designed for a non-sailing purpose. How long you make the line will depend on how far you want them to be able to move, but ideally it should be short enough to prevent them going under the water should they fall overboard. A harness need not be so awful to wear, and should stop a child falling overboard in the first place.

Children are probably less aware of the risk of hurting themselves, so you need to keep an eye open until you are confident of what they can do. They may be better at making their way around a yacht than adults, but climbing down the companionway steps or getting ashore can be more difficult if they are small.

Walking down steps backwards is usually easier, and getting on and off may need a hand. Dinghies have the irritating habit of moving away as you get into them, and children may need help when getting in and out. Passing a small child to an adult already in a dinghy is better than trying to carry the child with you.

Under fives

Many families deliberate over the age at which small children should be taken on a sailing holiday abroad, especially if none of the family has been on this type of holiday before. We have seen a number of young and even very young children taken successfully on this type of holiday, though you may prefer to try just one week afloat for the first time. Remember that if there are only two adults on board, a small child may monopolise one while the other copes with everything else singlehanded.

Climate is more important where very young children are concerned, and you may need to pick the time of year you go more carefully. Lack of heating on board will not normally be a problem, though you may want to avoid times when it might be damp, such as very early season in the Mediterranean.

Charter yachts are rarely designed with small children in mind, and sleeping arrangements need to be considered. Leecloths (collapsible bunk sides)

What flotilla is all about. A day's freedom, followed by a rendez-vous in a secluded anchorage to make sailing friends.

help keep a child in a bunk when sailing as well as at other times, but there may not be any as holiday charter yachts are rarely kitted out for long passages. Bags or cushions on the floor should help prevent them coming to any real harm if they do fall out, but you need to take great care while sailing.

Some crewed charters may be able to supply you with cots or chairs for very young children, but your average bareboat or flotilla yacht will not, so you are unlikely to enjoy the facilities you are used to at home. Taking everything with you is not practical, but some items could make your life easier, such as a lightweight buggy, or car seat for a very young child which perhaps could be strapped somewhere safe when sailing and also used at meal times. Think about what you use at home, how you might improvise, and what you cannot do without. It may help to have a look at a similar yacht beforehand to get an idea of what it will be like and what you should take, perhaps at a boat show where such yachts will be on display.

Toddlers need a good eye on them above and below decks. Cookers on gimbals present a hazard, and movements of the boat can tip the best of us off balance. There may well be times when you are not able to keep an eye on them, such as when putting up the sails, and the last thing you want to find is that they have climbed the companionway steps and reached the deck without putting on a lifejacket or harness.

If a small child has specific dietary needs such as semi-solid food, you may be able to buy ready prepared foods where you go or may prefer to take a few packets or jars along as standbys. Dried or packaged foods are less likely to cause a problem with customs than fresh food. Bottled mineral water is available in most places, but you may want to take some means of treating water if there is any doubt.

A little more thought will need to be given to health care, such as what to take and what to do in the event of illness. It is a good idea to have some child strength Paracetamol in case of a raised temperature. Sponging down with tepid water is also a good way of reducing a fever. Calamine lotion can be useful for skin irritation or sunburn, but it is better to take ample measures to avoid them in the first place. Bouts of sickness and diarrhoea will need to be taken more seriously when in a hot climate due to the dangers of dehydration which young children are much less able to cope with. You should seek advice about vaccinations if courses are not yet completed, and a GP or health visitor may be able to give advice about health care for a young child whilst abroad.

FLOTILLAS
The myths

If we mention flotillas to anyone who has some knowledge of yacht charter, invariably their comments will include something about a 'mother duck' and how awful it must be to look after all those people who do not know what they are doing. These opinions highlight some misconceptions surrounding the concept of flotilla holidays, as well as some unhelpful attitudes held by those who consider themselves to be experienced.

It is true that many people go on flotilla to gain experience. It certainly is not true to say that no one knows what they are doing. People can join a flotilla with a vast range of knowledge and experience for many different reasons. Some have their own yachts at home, and some have been sailing all their lives in areas that demand respect such as the Irish Sea. Whilst it might have been true in the past that yachts in a flotilla followed a leader from place to place, nowadays it is rare to find a flotilla that operates on such restrictive lines. Some are designed to be that way for novice sailors, but on the majority people are free to do as they please during the day, the only requirement being to meet up with the rest of the flotilla in the evening. Some companies have even sought to find an alternative name for their flotillas in an attempt to get away from the old attitudes.

Who goes and why?

The main reasons people seem to choose a flotilla holiday are because they are easy, because they lack sufficient experience to go bareboat, and for the social aspect.

Inexperience need not be confined to lack of sailing experience. It can often be that an unfamiliar area and yacht will cause people to choose a flotilla holiday as opposed to bareboat charter. A skipper may be very good at boat handling and mooring in a familiar area, but have no knowledge or experience of bows-to or stern-to mooring and a larger yacht that may require new handling skills.

Gaining theoretical knowledge may be relatively easy, but practical skills are not as easy to come by, especially as skipper. To guarantee being able to skipper a yacht at home it will usually be necessary to own one. Sailing school courses allow you to gain experience, but it can become an expensive way of doing so if there are no other opportunities. Flotilla holidays are an excellent opportunity to gain valuable experience both as skipper and crew, and to improve boat handling skills. Even if they are non-tidal waters,

Life's a beach, and the barbecue is traditional on any flotilla holiday. It's prepared and cooked by the support crew, with as much help as the charterers want to give.

sea miles will still count towards recognised qualifications. Experience gained on flotilla often allows people to charter a bareboat yacht subsequently.

Socially, flotillas can add a great deal to the enjoyment of a holiday. Activities are organised to give opportunities to meet the other members of the flotilla, such as a drinks party on the beach and evening events such as a meal together in a local restaurant at the beginning and end of the holiday. Some may even organise trips to places of interest either inland or offshore, such as an area where snorkelling is particularly good or a site of historical interest. Many flotillas arrange an informal race on or near the last day. None of these events will be obligatory.

Families with children and teenagers are often attracted to flotillas for the social aspect, though are often limited by school holidays. Some flotillas cater for the needs of single people by offering yacht share options. Occasionally a particular emphasis is placed on the social aspect if yachts are predominantly shared.

Life on flotilla

One week flotillas will obviously not be able to offer as large a cruising area as those of two weeks, and there will be less time available for what is known as free or independent sailing, where evenings as well as days are spent away from the flotilla. The flotilla crew are still available if needed, and give advice beforehand about places to go and any other information that might be helpful. They may also want to keep a record of which route each crew plans to take, in case they need to contact them for any reason such as a strong weather warning. Some may ask for daily VHF radio checks.

Before setting out each day, there will be a briefing about where the flotilla will be meeting in the evening, how to get there, and any relevant information about what there is on the way including possible shopping and lunch stops. It is quite acceptable to ask questions at these briefings, and flotilla staff can always be approached individually if you do not feel able to ask at the briefing itself.

The flotilla staff will normally spend more time in the first few days making sure crews are able to cope with mooring and leaving a mooring, so they will normally be the last to leave in the morning and will be standing on the quay ready to take your mooring lines. As the holiday progresses they will then give more freedom, maintaining a listening watch on the VHF throughout each day.

Crews are normally given a time by which the flotilla staff would like them to be in at the end of the day. This is usually early evening, though it will also be influenced by when the sun starts to go down. If crews think they will be in later than agreed, it is helpful if they can inform their flotilla crew. If anyone has a problem and realises they will not make it in before dark, the flotilla crew like to know so they can come out and help. Navigation at night in these areas is often difficult, and staying out late is not advised.

Days on flotilla will be much the same as on bareboat charter, with options such as whether or where to stop for lunch, whether to spend any time ashore, whether to sail all day or go straight there, and whether to allow any time for other activities such as snorkelling and windsurfing. The difference on bareboat charter is only that you can decide to stay put for the day should you want to, though this is still the option on flotilla free-sailing. Once the flotilla briefing is over, you will normally be free to set off when you please.

Group meals may or may not include a set menu, and will normally be at a restaurant that gives good value and is reliable. Flotillas are known for using and recommending certain restaurants, and this is usually because they can cope with the numbers of people, do not overcharge, and are consistent with the meals they provide as well as having other facilities such as showers and fresh water supplies. Some will also put on entertainment such as Greek dancing.

A punch party is usually arranged towards the start of the holiday, when people have begun to relax and are keen to start enjoying themselves. Barbecues are fairly relaxed affairs, and you may even be asked to contribute to the food. As regards entertainment, if you have awful visions of being dragged up to offer some sort of skit after eating, this is not obligatory and only takes place if people are there who like entertaining or acting the fool in public. Some people bring a musical instrument such as a guitar. If you do, make sure it will travel well and will not be disturbed by the heat and salty marine environment.

Each flotilla tends to develop its own character. Some are more sedate, and others are fairly lively. The fact that people are free to do their own thing means you can take it or leave it, and do not have to be put off by talk of social events. The common interest in sailing means there is usually someone you can get on with.

3 Where To Go?

In theory it is possible to have a sailing holiday almost anywhere in the world. You do not have to leave Britain to go on a crewed or bareboat charter and possibly even a flotilla. France's Brittany Coast has plenty to offer. There are adventure charters across the North Sea to Scandinavia and up inside the Arctic Circle. You can do Atlantic crossings, explore islands in the Pacific Ocean such as Polynesia and the Galapagos Islands, and cruise in the Red Sea. Many of these charters offer other attractions such as sub aqua diving.

Obviously those areas that are best suited will have the most significant numbers of charter yachts. Some areas are popular cruising grounds, but are restrictive to Europeans by virtue of the time and cost it takes to get there. New Zealanders are known for their love of sailing, and the Bay of Islands on its North Island is one of the most popular attractions. The Whitsunday Islands on the East Coast of Australia are protected by the Great Barrier Reef and afford safe cruising. It is possible to charter around islands in the South Pacific such as Fiji and Tahiti, or visit Mexico's Sea of Cortez, or Florida's West Coast. Thailand's Andaman Sea on its south-west coast is becoming more popular, with yachts available year-round for both bareboat charter and on flotilla. However, the vast majority of Europeans who go abroad to charter go to the Mediterranean and the Caribbean.

THE MEDITERRANEAN

The Mediterranean is popular with Europeans, with a wealth of areas to visit suiting all levels of experience that are near enough to home to make them easily accessible. There are a large number of holidays on offer, mainly advertised in yachting publications, but occasionally through high street travel agents and other travel publications.

Greece and Turkey

The majority of bareboat charters and flotillas are to be found in Greece and Turkey, but you can also charter on the south coast of France, particularly the Cote d'Azur, Corsica and Sardinia, the Tuscan islands including Elba, islands off the Bay of Naples including Capri on the west coast of Italy, and Spain's Balearic Islands. France and Italy are known for their good cuisine, though prices are generally higher than further east in the Mediterranean, and mooring fees need to be taken into consideration when working out the holiday budget. The weather and sailing conditions in the western Mediterranean are not as dependable as in Greece and Turkey, which are also blessed with numerous small harbours and anchorages, the majority of which cost nothing at all to stay in overnight.

As a final note, for those hoping to visit Turkey when chartering from Greece and visa versa, it may be possible for a Greek registered yacht to visit Turkey as long as a cruising permit is obtained, but it is not normally possible the other way around.

When to go

Charter in the Mediterranean is seasonal, starting around April and finishing by the end of October or early November. The further east you go the hotter it tends to be, and charters can start a little earlier and finish later. Weather at either end of the season can be changeable. In Greece it settles down around mid-May and often earlier in Turkey. October can be unsettled. This does not mean that periods of strong winds will not be experienced during the summer months, but they are much less likely than in very early or late season. Low season does have other advantages such as being cheaper, cooler and quieter.

There are several areas available for charter in Greece, mainly the Ionian, the Saronic and Argolic Gulfs, Chalkidiki, the Sporades, the West and South Peloponnese, the Cyclades and the Dodecanese. In Turkey the south-west Coast offers much in the way of interesting coastline, including the Dorian Gulf, the Lycian Coast, and the Gulfs of Gokova and Gulluck which are favourite areas.

Strong winds?

A variety of prevailing winds affect the eastern Mediterranean, some light and some much stronger. This means that some areas are more suited to inexperienced sailors than others. The Ionian Sea for example tends to be subject to a light to moderate north-westerly wind mostly in the afternoons which tends to die off in the evenings, though occasionally there may be periods of stronger southerlies. Winds in the Saronics are also fairly moderate, and those in the Sporades a little stronger. The central and eastern part of the Aegean which includes the Cyclades, Dodecanese and the Turkish coast are subjected to stronger winds, being affected during the summer months by the north or north-westerly wind known as the Meltemi that becomes more westerly as it travels along the Turkish coast. It starts to build during June, is generally strongest during July and August when it is sometimes as much as force seven, and falls off again during September. Stronger winds means that you will not find these areas recommended for inexperienced sailors.

Areas such as the South of France and Italian coast can be affected by swells that build up from other parts of the Mediterranean. A westerly gale in the Golfe du Lion for example causes a large swell on the west coast of Corsica. This is much more of a swell than areas such as Greece and Turkey where strong prevailing winds will tend to produce a short, choppy sea of quite different character.

THE CARIBBEAN

The Caribbean Sea is far larger than the area normally promoted for yacht charter. It stretches as far as Venezuela in the south, Cuba and Puerto Rico in the north, and Central America in the west. To the east lies an arc of islands that we usually think of as the Caribbean, that can be divided into the Virgin Islands and the Leeward and Windward Islands. The Leewards and Windwards are also known as the Lesser Antilles. The Bahamas lie outside the Caribbean Sea, in the Atlantic Ocean to the north.

There is an enormous variety of geography and culture as well as nationality, forms of government, racial background and language throughout the Caribbean. All kinds of multinational influences have played their part in creating this variety. Some islands still retain connections with the European powers that once occupied them, and some are now totally independent.

The Windward Islands for example are in fact four

The Mediterranean is the favourite choice for European charterers. The British actually invented the concept of flotilla holidays in Greece, and it is still the number one destination. This is Parga, a typical overnight stop for flotillas and bareboat yachts in the area.

countries in total. The Virgin Islands are split into the British Virgin Islands, the main one of which is Tortola, and the US Virgin Islands which are now part of the United States. Some islands are known for the beauty of the landscape and the variety of wildlife. Some are more sparse, and many have beautiful beaches and coral reefs, offering exciting snorkelling and sub aqua diving.

The Virgin Islands

The Virgin Islands are a popular centre for yacht charter, being sheltered, and therefore more suitable for the less experienced than the Windwards or Leewards. Steady trade winds and a year-round warm climate throughout the Eastern Caribbean make it an ideal cruising ground. From November to January winds are usually from the north-east and between

The Caribbean promises excellent sailing during the winter. This is Sandy Cay, with a flotilla lying out at anchor.

about force four and force six. Exposed northern shores can also be affected by swells caused by winter storms in the Atlantic at this time. In the summer between February and October the wind tends to be south-easterly and lighter. There may be occasional showers or odd days of rain, February to June being the drier season.

Hurricane time

The hurricane season in the Caribbean lasts from June to October, the most likely time for them to occur being in August and September. Forecasting is generally good and there are places to hide if a hurricane is known to be approaching. Some parts may be more seriously affected, though most places are at risk. Terms used in forecasts concerning tropical weather may not be ones you are familiar with. Charters are still available all year round, and companies vary as to how much they make of the hurricane risk within their holiday literature.

The Bahamas

The weather in the Bahamas is less predictable, being affected by weather from the United States, and winters are not as warm. Tidal waters mean that greater navigational skills are required than for the Caribbean, where tidal effects are often minimal.

4 Protecting Your Holiday

It is not always possible to be sure that no disaster will befall a holiday once it is booked. Companies do go bust, and airlines fold. There are ways to make sure your holiday is well protected against such things, and a few things to consider when reading the small print which should tell you what a company will do in the event of a problem such as failed expectations and engine breakdown, and about your commitments if you decide to cancel.

Responsibility

We have used the term 'charter company' fairly liberally throughout this book as a kind of all-encompassing term, even though often it would have been more accurate to be specific about which part of the operation was being referred to at that particular time. The problem is that sailing holiday companies operate in different ways.

There are three basic parts to a charter operation: the part that takes care of bookings and travel arrangements, the part that owns the yachts or facilities, and the part that manages them. They do not necessarily all belong to the same company. Some owners for example use a booking agent or travel agent to organise their flights and bookings who may have very little responsibility once the basic booking is done. Others will use a company to book their yachts or facilities who are the principal party when it comes to responsibility to the client. Some companies will organise the booking side of the operation themselves. Some own the yachts, and some manage them for others or perhaps have a mixture of the two. Some may be individual outfits, and some large concerns.

Companies may be bound by restrictions placed on them by the country in which their yachts or operations are based, such as who is allowed to have ownership and in which country the yacht must be registered, and most importantly in how much protection is given to charterers. There are EC regulations governing package holidays for example. In the end there may or may not be a difference in the service you receive, but there could be in the extent to which your holiday is protected against such eventualities as your damaging another person or their property while sailing, or if the company fails while you are out there.

So there are a few things to look at before committing yourselves and your money to paper. Again we have tended to concentrate on sailing yacht charter, but the same applies to whatever kind of charter it is, plus dinghy and windsurfing holidays.

PRIME CONCERNS

There a five areas you should look at when enquiring about a holiday to see if you are going to be fully covered. These are marine insurance, third party insurance, public indemnity/liability insurance, bonding and booking conditions. In addition there is individual holiday insurance, which companies may insist you have before booking one of their holidays.

Insurance liability

The owner of a yacht is going to want to know that it will be covered for any damage or loss incurred while it is out on charter. This is often referred to as marine insurance, and a company should tell you if yachts are fully covered. An individual owner for example could risk letting payments slip if they are having financial problems, and cover should therefore be written into any agreement you sign. You must also check third party insurance, to cover any damage caused to another person or their property by you while on the yacht, dinghy or windsurfer as appropriate.

Public liability included in personal holiday insurance will not be an adequate alternative. Security deposits or security insurance cover the first part of any claim which is not paid by the insurers. Make sure that this is the limit of your responsibility and that you will not be asked to pay for anything else. It is important that résumés of past experience are accurate so as not to give insurers a reason for disallowing a claim.

Everything is right with the world - or is it? The last thing you want to find out is that the charter company has folded, and the police are waiting on the quay ready to impound your yacht.

Public indemnity or liability insurance concerns the company responsibility towards others. This will cover clients for any injury or loss incurred for which the company may be held responsible. This for example would include an accident suffered while travelling on transport that has been arranged by them. Being in possession of this insurance is not a legal requirement for charter companies.

Bonding

Bonding is a means of protecting clients from charter company or airline failure. All EC companies that sell travel-inclusive holidays are required by law to be bonded. For flight-inclusive holidays they must put forward a sum of money as a bond with the CAA, which then issues an Air Travel Organisers Licence (ATOL). This bond covers refunds for flights or repatriation if the charter company or airline fold. It will also cover other aspects of the holiday such as the charter price of the yacht, if it was sold as flight-inclusive. Organisations such as the Association of British Travel Agents (ABTA) and the Association of

Independent Tour Operators Trust (AITO) give protection to charterers for non-flight inclusive holidays and for other aspects of the holiday through bonding, which may include items such as payments towards legal costs. Non-package holidays will not be protected if the company holds no other bonds. Details of any bonding a company has is normally included somewhere in its literature, on the back page or with information such as booking or charter conditions.

Bonded companies ensure that insurance is adequate. If a company sells a holiday and is not bonded, or you book it yourself through a brochure sent from abroad, you need to be careful about how the yachts and yourselves are covered with regards to marine and third party insurance, and public liability insurance. Paying by Access or Visa gives you additional protection against company failure, although this will not cover repatriation, etc., which ATOL, ABTA and AITO do.

The small print

Included in many brochures are a few pages of small print, usually entitled 'booking' or 'charter conditions', or sometimes 'general information'. These will include all manner of items such as what will happen in the event of the charterer wanting to cancel, responsibility if a yacht is not available when you get there or if days of sailing are lost through mechanical breakdown, complaints procedures, and what happens if you do not return the yacht by the agreed time.

It is important to know where you stand if things do not meet expectations. This is where you should also find information about marine and other forms of insurance. Companies are not legally required to have booking conditions, and if there is nothing written when you sign an agreement, then they cannot be held responsible if things go wrong. Just as important as what a company will do, is what it will not do, as they vary in what they consider to be their responsibility to the client. For companies to be ATOL, ABTA or AITO bonded, they will need to have booking or charter agreements that meet with the approval of the regulatory body, who scrutinise the wording of company brochures.

Flight packages

When buying a flight-inclusive package, it is essential to make sure that the company selling it to you holds an ATOL. To make sure your flight is protected, you need to be issued with a receipt that has an ATOL number. Non-charter flights are not protected by ATOL bonding.

Own travel

If you wish to make your own travel arrangements, and opt for scheduled or APEX flights you can be protected from airline failure by paying for them with a credit card such as Access or Visa. There are cheaper scheduled flights, sold early and without the option to make alterations if you change your mind about when you want to travel. If you obtain a flight through a newspaper advert for example, find out what kind of a flight it is and therefore if any protection is offered, and make sure you have an ATOL receipt for any charter flight.

Holiday insurance

Personal holiday insurance normally covers medical expenses (including repatriation and hospital benefits), personal accident, personal liability, luggage and money (which usually includes a daily payment for delayed luggage, travel delay and disruption which may include missed flights), and cancellation and curtailment (due to accident, illness or redundancy). Make sure that your insurance allows for the sailing and the other watersports activities you intend to do.

Many companies offer travel insurance, and it is normally paid for at the time of booking along with a deposit so as to cover cancellations, but it is of course non-refundable if you change your mind and cancel the holiday. There are often reduced premiums for children, and ages and amounts do vary. It may be obligatory to have personal insurance when travelling by charter flight.

Other protection

Other forms of holiday protection include having an E111 form to cover some medical expenses if you do not have holiday insurance. Paying for holidays with certain types of credit card may provide some holiday insurance.

Visa requirements

As a final point it is important that all crew fulfil any necessary visa requirements, and that all passports will be valid for the length of stay. Some countries ask that they be valid for a period of six months afterwards as well. Some visas are obtained as you enter the country, and you will need to ensure you have the appropriate means of payment.

5 What Do You Really Want?

Here is a checklist of questions to ask to help decide what you want from a holiday, and which will be the most suitable.

The yacht
- What size?
- How many berths?
- Do you want space or is the number you take determined by a budget?
- Do you want to be able to get to the heads in the night without having to make it past those asleep in the saloon?
- Do you want separate heads if there are two couples sharing?
- What berth lengths and widths do you need?
- Will the forepeak have enough legroom for the two people who plan to sleep there?
- Do you need separate cabins for children?
- Will those in the aft cabin be kept awake by partying in the cockpit?
- How big are the cabins, and can they be shut off from the saloon?

Yourself
- What size of boat can you handle?
- How many crew have you available?
- What are their experience and abilities?
- What is your previous experiences as skipper?
- How much agility is required?

The yacht's features
- Does the yacht need to be user-friendly?
- Do you want an easy-to handle mainsail with lazy jacks or roller furling?
- Do you need a bow anchor winch, manual or electric?
- Fridge or cool-box? Shower or hot water?
- Capacities of water and fuel?
- Wheel or tiller?

The yacht's inventory
- What comes as standard and what is an optional extra on board?
- Cruising chute, outboard engine, autopilot, snorkelling equipment, sun awning, bed linen and towels?
- How much local information is supplied by pilot guides?

Optional extras
- Do you need them and will you use them? Do you need a windsurfer? Flotillas usually carry one for general use.

What design?
- Sail or motor?
- Exciting to sail or steady?
- Does it need to be good for families, with a swim platform on the stern?

How old is the yacht?
- This is not necessarily going to tell you much about its state of repair, which will depend on how well it has been maintained. Some companies however will offer the option to choose between different ages of yacht, newer ones being more expensive.

What is not included in the basic price?
- Mooring fees, fuel, security deposit or security insurance, optional extras, cleaning at the end of the holiday, transfers, cruising permit, holiday insurance? Some of these may be different depending on whether it is bareboat charter or flotilla. Items such as mooring fees and permits will vary considerably depending on the area.

Travel arrangements and transfers
- What is involved?
- Can you fly from a chosen airport?
- How long will it take to get there?
- Is it all arranged for you or are you expected to

make your own way to and from the airport?

Flotilla

- One or two weeks?
- One way or return trip?
- How many free sailing days? There are considerable variations between flotillas, some having one or two days,and some more than a week.
- Length of daily passages?
- Yacht share options if required?
- Do you need tuition?
- Are you going to be a frustrated bareboater?

Bareboat

- Suitable for what level of expertise?
- How much support do you want/need?
- What does the company provide in the way of back-up services?
- Do you want to be able to link with a flotilla in the area?
- Round trip or one way? There can be a supplement for a one way trip.

Crewed charter

- Do you want a bareboat with skipper or crew, or a fully crewed yacht?
- Do you want to DIY, or to be wined and dined?
- Do you want luxury and space, or just to be comfortable and friendly?
- Who owns the yacht?
- Who are the skipper and crew?
- Do you want other activities such as windsurfing, sub-aqua or water-skiing?
- Do you want the yacht to yourselves or to join others on something larger such as a Gulet in Turkey (a traditional motor sailor)?
- Do you want to sail or doesn't it matter?

Combination holidays

- Do you want to spend the whole holiday afloat? If not what else do you want to do?
- Do you want just a villa or would you like organised activities?
- Do you want sailing instruction, or to learn something new?
- Do you want specialised activities for children?

The social aspect

- Do you want to meet other people?
- Do you want any organised events?
- If you are a crew of two couples, and there are

Is this yacht the right size and shape for you? Are you in the right location? Is the weather what you expected? Think out your requirements, and then see what the charter companies have on offer.

likely to be disagreements about who is the boss, might it be a better option to take two smaller yachts instead?

Climate and weather

- Must it be hot or not too hot?
- Preferred sailing conditions? How much wind? Calm seas?

What the crew want to do

- Do you all want the same things – the same time spent on the water, the same sightseeing, the same degree of sailing difficulty? There may be a need to compromise, especially if the crew do not normally sail together.
- What considerations do you need to make for children?

Eating out

- Must you be able to eat out, or do you want to self-cater and if so how much?
- How expensive will it be to eat out?

Health needs

- Any specific problems?

PART TWO

SAILING AS
SKIPPER OR CREW

6 The Yacht

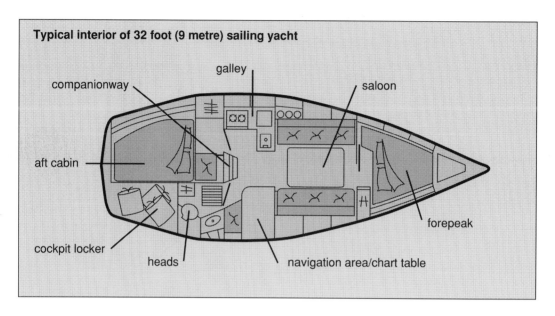

Typical interior of 32 foot (9 metre) sailing yacht

galley

companionway

saloon

aft cabin

forepeak

cockpit locker

heads

navigation area/chart table

Most modern yachts have comfortable seating areas that double up as sleeping accomodation. Saloon tables frequently fold away to make room for an in-fill to extend the seating into a double berth. Other bunks are in cabins such as the forepeak and aft cabin. The larger the yacht, the more people it will be able to accommodate, unless the emphasis is on luxury

The comfortable interior of a small modern yacht. Never pack in too many people. A yacht this size should be about right for two adults and two children.

charter. It may seem unnecessary to say check the accomodation when you arrive, but we had an Italian couple on flotilla who spent the entire fortnight on separate bunks, not realising they converted to a double. She was upset, but he said he needed the sleep!

Water systems

Check out where the tank is and if there is a fullness gauge. Notice where the filler cap is on deck and make sure you know where it is in relation to the diesel filler, because the two must never be mixed. Either liquid in the wrong place will cause serious problems. To fill the water tank(s), use a hose or jerrycan and funnel. When it seems to be full, wait a few moments to let any air escape and try a bit more. When the tank is full, water will either start to drain out of the taps, or from an overflow (usually nearby). Do not leave it unattended or you could fill the sinks and galley, or worse still the boat.

Water is pumped from tank to taps by manually operated (foot or hand) or electrically powered

Never muddle water and diesel! In hot countries water is scarce, so take care not to overfill and waste a precious commodity.

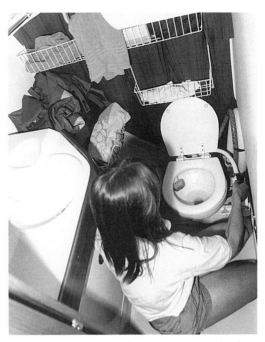

The heads compartment is by its nature cramped, unless you are on an enormous yacht. If anyone needs to use it when you are under way, make sure they have sufficient ventilation. It is often not a good place to be seasick. Better to do that over the side.

pumps. An electrically pressurized water system will often be supplemented by a manual pump in case of loss of electrical power. Electric pumps can burn out if allowed to run dry, and it is a good idea to turn them off on the electrical panel when not in use. Some yachts have a sea water tap to help conserve fresh water. In theory washing up can be done in sea water and rinsed with fresh afterwards, but it is not really advisable in many harbours and marinas. Some taps can be used for both and need switching over as required.

Waste water travels via piping to the sea outside. In some countries discharge of this grey water into

Make sure you know where the seacocks are and how to turn them off and on. This is the on position, with the handle pointing along the pipe

inland waterways is illegal, in which case there should be a tank into which it is discharged. Turkey is particularly concerned about what is discharged into the sea, and may require waste water to be pumped into the holding tank via the toilet.

Sometimes with the boat on a heel, seawater will flow back up the pipe and into the sink. This can be prevented by turning off the seacock at the bottom of the pipe before sailing. Many advise that all seacocks on sink drains, toilet intakes and outflows are turned off before any journey is made to minimise danger of taking in water through the hull fittings in the event of a damaged pipe. If you do this, make sure NOT to turn off the seacocks on the engine cooling water intake or the cockpit drains.

Heads

Toilets on boats are otherwise known as the heads. Perhaps when women were a rarer presence, less consideration was given to comfort. Undressing and sitting down with the door closed is a virtual impossibility in some older, smaller yachts. Newer designs allow a little (if not a lot) more space in the smallest room.

The end of the bilge pump hose under the floorboards. Some residual water will always be left behind. On a modern yacht the bilges are likely to be very shallow.

Although some motor yachts and those designed for the inland waterways are able to use toilet plumbing similar to that found on shore, sailing yachts are not. The marine toilet is operated by pumping water in and out. To flush, seawater is pumped in via a fitting in the hull and then out again via another fitting, or into a holding tank from where it is pumped out later. Normally this will be into the sea a few miles from shore. On inland waterways it is often at a pumping out station. Holding tanks are compulsory on many charter yachts such as those in Turkey, and it is important to find out where it is acceptable to pump them out. Some areas such as the US Virgin Islands require that the waste is macerated and treated in the tank first. Systems therefore vary and you will need to be briefed on the peculiarities of the one you have on board.

Toilet operation

To operate a conventional manually operated marine toilet, first make sure the seacocks are turned on.

Some pumps are double action, pumping water in on one stroke and waste out on the next. There will also be a lever or switch to enable the water intake to be turned off and therefore empty the bowl. In this case select the pump-out position and pump several times to clear the bowl. Switch the lever over and pump again to flush. Use the pump-out position again to empty the bowl. Sometimes two separate pumps are used, and some toilets make use of the pump that pumps waste out and a sealable lid on the bowl to create suction to draw the flushing water in. The lid therefore must be closed before flushing. Pump with the handle 8 to 10 times, wait 5 seconds or so, and pump again around 6 times. Suction will prevent you from opening the lid for a little while. Electrically operated toilet pumps have simple push button controls.

Toilets that discharge directly outside are usually able to cope with small amounts of soft toilet paper. Holding tanks however are prone to blockages if paper is used. Keep a plastic bag for waste paper by the side of the toilet, and unless you are advised otherwise do not put anything down the toilet that you have not eaten first! An additional pump will be used to empty the holding tank. Keep pumping until you feel the handle become more free. It is fairly safe to say that pumping out the tank once a day will prevent any overflows.

Some toilet cleaners can cause damage to the pipes, and you may be asked only to use a certain type such as one that is alkali based.

Showers

You may find a shower incorporated into the sink unit in the heads. It may be part of the electrically pressurized system, or operated with a foot pump. Waste water may need to be mopped or pumped out from under the floorboards, or may drain down into the bilges to be pumped out from there.

You may prefer to shower on deck instead. Solar showers are frequently provided, and some yachts have a deck shower incorporated into the pressurized system. Many yachts, more usually larger ones, have systems that make use of the engine to provide hot water.

The bilges

You will find the bilges beneath the floorboards. Water can sometimes seep into a boat from places such as around the seal where the propeller shaft goes through the hull (stern gland), and a little water in the bilges is nothing to be alarmed about. Bilge pumps are used to pump out any water that collects but they are unable to get rid of it totally, because air gets into the system as the water level goes down. Pumps can be manual or electric, and sometimes automatic. Water in the bilges, especially if they are shallow, can find its way into lockers low down. Keep the bilges dry, and sponge them out if necessary. Be careful where you stow things that need to be kept dry.

The galley

The kitchen or galley may not be as spacious or as well equipped as the one at home, but should be adequate for a two week holiday. At the least you can expect a two ring gas stove, and perhaps additionally a grill and/or oven. The gas cylinder (and also hopefully a spare) will usually be in a locker in the

The smaller the galley, the neater you need to be. Most small yachts are fitted with a drainable insulated cold box that can be chilled by packing with ice packs or ice to keep provisions cool. Do not expect to find a fridge on a yacht of this size.

The best place for the gas bottle is outside the galley in the cockpit locker. It should be turned off when not in use, and if treated sensibly is a very safe form of cooking fuel.

cockpit. Gas will sink if it escapes, and the locker should have an outlet pipe to the outside of the boat to prevent gas leaking into the bilges where it is an explosive risk. Many gas cookers will have a thermocouple on the burners to prevent the gas being on but not lit. To light the burners, press in and turn the knob. Light the gas and hold the knob in for about 5 seconds. The gas will be cut off if the knob is released before the thermocouple has heated up.

Many cookers will be on gimbals so as to swing and remain horizontal as you sail. With fiddles on the cooker top to hold pans in place, this enables you to cook (or at least boil a kettle!) en route. Switch the gas supply off at the top of the cylinder when not in use. If there is a gas leak into the boat, use the bilge pump to pump it outside.

Fridges are becoming an increasingly common feature on charter yachts, though many still have only a cool box. Blocks of ice or frozen plastic bottles of water can sometimes be put in the cool box to keep the beer cold. As the ice melts, it will drain into a container or the bilges, or collect in the bottom of the box. Fridges work on the same principle as normal domestic ones.

All fridges are only as good as the power behind them. Most run off a battery, though some are engine driven or may use a generator or shore power. Very occasionally they are driven by gas. Sometimes the yacht will have a large battery capacity, allowing the fridge to be kept on for longer periods, which you should be advised of at the initial briefing. On others, it will be necessary to turn the fridge off when the engine is off, or it may be too great a drain on the batteries. You may still need to resort to ice. Freezers are often available on larger (usually crewed) yachts, having the power supplies needed to operate them.

Batteries

The batteries on a boat are usually 12 volt, as in a car. More often than not there will be two, one dedicated to starting the engine, and one to everything else such as the cabin lights, navigation lights, navigation instruments and fridge. Make sure you know how and when to turn the batteries on and off. Lights, instruments, fridge, water and bilge pumps and other electrical items will usually need to be turned on at a switch on the electrical control panel as well as on the appliance itself. One switch will control all the cabin lights for example. Some control panels are far more complex than others.

Navigation

Most yachts have an area specifically for use when navigating. The chart table can usually be lifted to reveal a space underneath for charts, pilot guides (information about harbours and the area), and other navigational equipment. Some small yachts have a fold-down or slide-out chart table to allow more room in the saloon.

A variety of electronic instruments may be on board such as a log to measure speed and distance travelled, echo sounder to measure the depth of the

Only large yachts will have a full size chart table. Some small yachts simply make do with the saloon table. In either case, all the navigational equipment should be kept together.

sea bed below, instruments to measure the strength and direction of the wind, and VHF radio to receive and transmit messages. Some, usually more expensive, charters will have a global positioning system (GPS) on board.

LOOKING AFTER YOUR YACHT
Hatches

When it is hot, you may not feel like battening down the hatches every time you set sail, but it is a good idea to close them before leaving the quay even if the sea looks calm. The situation may be different when you get out and start sailing, and the wake from a passing ferry can take you by surprise and swamp the forepeak cushions.

Do not swab the decks with a hatch even slightly open or you will have to sleep on damp bunks. Some hatches have two shut positions. One leaves the hatch open slightly to allow a little ventilation. Make sure you use the other one. Avoid taking interior cushions out on deck or they will be even wetter if they go overboard.

Stowage

Cupboards and lockers are fitted with catches to prevent them opening as the boat moves about. Stow everything away before you set off to prevent spills and breakages from things flying about.

Cleaning and care

No one wants to spend their holiday cleaning, but it is a good idea to try to keep the boat in some sort of order. Rubbish and food attract flies and wasps, so clear them away when you can. Be careful not to mark or damage floorboards with the wrong kind of footwear, and take care not to damage work surfaces when cutting. Repairs such as these will usually have to be left to the end of the season as there will be no time between charters. Avoid putting cups of coffee or glasses of wine down on the chart table or worse still the charts themselves, or you may not be able to see where you are going the next day. When en route, keep charts and pilot guides inside.

Awnings

Sun awnings should be taken in at night and when travelling. The wind can cause damage, and at night the awning can act like a sail and cause your anchor to

Check that the hatches are properly closed before a wave breaks over the bow and drenches the forepeak or saloon.

drag. Bimini tops, often found on boats in the Caribbean, are a more permanent affair and can be left in situ.

The dinghy

Charter regulations may mean that you will be asked to keep your dinghy inflated at all times (unless it is a rigid tender in which case there will probably be somewhere specific to stow it on deck). Make sure it is always left well tied on. In calm weather (unless you are advised otherwise) it is usually OK to have it trailing behind the boat. When it is windy, keep it tied on deck using several anchor points, otherwise it may flip over in the wind, perhaps several times, and you risk losing the dinghy if the painter is torn out.

If you hire, or are provided with an outboard engine for the tender, there will usually be a bracket mounted on the stern rail of the yacht on which to keep it when not in use. Do not tow an inflatable dinghy with the outboard attached or it will be submerged if the dinghy turns over. For the same reason, do not leave the oars on board as they are frequently lost this way. Take the outboard off at night because as it gets cooler, the dinghy becomes less rigid as the air pressure inside decreases, and therefore less able to support the outboard which may be semi-submerged in the morning.

An inflatable tender is an expensive item. Don't leave it behind, and make sure it is properly secure.

7 Boat Etiquette

Read on, because here are a few hints on how to make yourself popular that you may not have thought of previously.

• Try and have a little patience with those around you. Stress and lack of confidence can cause people to act in surprising ways, such as when coming into a harbour or sailing with the family for the first time. It takes many of us a while to settle down to being on holiday. You may have a lower opinion of some nations than others, but try to keep an open mind and make an effort to communicate.

• Noise is often one of the things we go on holiday to avoid. There may be nothing to be done about the noisy quayside bar or disco apart from buying earplugs, but annoying our neighbours (and perhaps the entire harbour) with partying on deck until the early hours is one way to get a bad name. Few want to spoil enjoyment by being a party pooper, but it has to work both ways. Remember that sound travels very well over water, and if you like to gossip be careful what you say!

• If you have lain in bed in the forepeak and listened to people stumbling over your decks on their slightly drunken way, you will know that it sounds something like the base section of a heavy metal band passing overhead. Every sound is amplified, so tread carefully. Although some enjoy the sound of halyards clanking against the mast, many do not. Try tying them away from the mast with a line around the shrouds.

• If you are lucky enough to have a generator on board, try to avoid using the washing machine in the evenings. Humming generators can be very difficult to sleep with.

• Try not to transmit over others when using the VHF radio, even if they do seem to be hogging the channel unnecessarily. Keeping down the number of calls made to raise another station will help prevent walking over another transmission without realising it, especially if using channel 16.

• Show respect for other boats and property, even if they look run-down and uncared for. The right to moor as and when you please cannot always be assumed, and take care not to cause damage to local boats or small quays whatever their condition. Many local boat owners are happy to share space with visiting yachts, but appreciate a little consideration.

• Always ask permission to go on another boat or tie on lines, and avoid leaving dirty footmarks on her decks.

• Boats are rarely closed up in warm climates and it is easy to inadvertently look down inside a companionway or hatch. If you have to cross a boat to get to your own, walk forward of the shrouds and not via the cockpit. Always make sure your fenders are where they should be, even if your neighbour seems to be in short supply.

• Keep as clear as you can of other people's anchor lines when coming in to moor. Don't make people nervous by cutting it too fine. They have no way of knowing how skilled you are. If you wrap someone's line around your propeller it will frequently be damaged if not cut in two.

Left: Show courtesy to local fishermen, ferries, taverna owners (many provide quay space and services for yachts) and private and charter boats alike.

8 Sailing - How It Works

Sailing is not just a matter of being pushed along by the wind in the sails, though it once used to be. Square-rigged trading ships carried large square areas of sail and ran before the wind, pushed along by the trade winds. Nowadays the same principal applies when sailing a yacht with the wind coming from behind, and sails such as the spinnaker have been designed to make use of wind from the stern.

So what happens when you want to sail with the wind coming from another direction such as on the side (beam), or forward of the beam? Sail shape and design have changed dramatically from the old square-rigger days, making it possible to sail into the wind as well as away from it.

The number and shape of sails will depend on the size and design of the yacht, but the configuration of main -sail and headsail (also known as foresail) is very common. The mainsail is supported by the mast, and the headsail by the forestay.

1

2

TACKING:

"Ready about". Get ready by making sure the headsail sheet in use is ready to be released and free to run. Put a couple of turns round the other winch with the new sheet.

The helmsman will indicate he is starting the tack by clearly saying "Le – oh!". As soon as the headsail starts to back, quickly release the sheet from the winch.

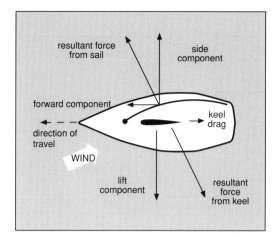

Wind flow

Just as an aeroplane is lifted into the air by the action of air passing over its wings, so a sailing yacht is driven through the water by wind flow over the sails. Because a sail is curved, wind passing over it creates a difference in air pressure between one side and the other. Lift is produced as air is drawn towards the area of lower pressure, and results in movement of the yacht through the water. When the wind is on the beam, this drive is forwards, and this is a very efficient point of sail. If the wind is forward of the beam (beating), some of the drive is forwards, but more is sideways and therefore less efficient. This sideways effect also causes the yacht to heel over.

Ballast and heeling over

Just as a bottle floats until allowed to fill with water, so a boat is buoyant due to the air trapped inside. Weight (ballast) in the bottom keeps the boat stable in the water. Sailing yachts have a heavy metal keel on the bottom which acts as a counter-balance to the effect of the wind on the sails, rather like one of those children's toys that refuses to lie down. Many inexperienced crews become very nervous when a

Pull in on the other sheet as quickly as you can, watching the sail as it changes sides to ensure it does not get caught on anything such as the shrouds.

Use the winch as soon as you are unable to pull the sheet in by hand. Wind the sheet in until the leech of the headsail is almost touching the spreaders.

POINTS OF SAIL

WIND

Beating

Beating is sailing as close as possible into the wind without stalling the sails. The upper limit in a cruising yacht is about 45 degrees off the wind's direction. If you attempt to point any higher into the wind, the yacht will slow right down. The sails are pulled in as tight as possible in moderate or strong winds, but not quite so tight if the wind is light.

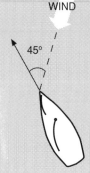

45°

WIND

WIND

Close Reach

Sailing with the wind just forward of the beam

Head To Wind

No yacht is able to sail directly into the wind. The only way it can make progress in that direction is with its engine on, or possibly with a strong tide underneath it. When the sails start to flap (with the wind blowing from the other side) it is time to bear away from the wind by pulling the tiller towards you. Otherwise you will come head to wind and stop.

WIND

Beam Reach

Sailing with the wind on the beam (side-on). On any reach the course should be set, and the sails let out until they just start to 'back' due to the wind hitting them from the other side. Then pull them in slightly for maximum power.

WIND

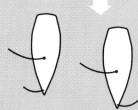

WIND

Running

Running is sailing with the wind behind. The sails are set almost at right angles to the boat, although this is usually limited by the shrouds which hold up the rig. On a 'dead run' with the wind directly behind, the headsail is blanketed by the mainsail and may need to be 'goosewinged' on the other side as shown.

Broad Reach

Sailing with the wind just behind the beam. This is generally a yacht's fastest and often most enjoyable point of sailing.

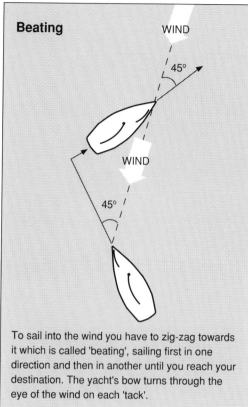

Beating

WIND

45°

WIND

45°

To sail into the wind you have to zig-zag towards it which is called 'beating', sailing first in one direction and then in another until you reach your destination. The yacht's bow turns through the eye of the wind on each 'tack'.

Gybing

WIND

A yacht gybes when it turns its stern through the eye of the wind. This manoeuvre is performed when running downwind. Take great care, since the boom can cross from side to side at tremendous speed. People have been knocked overboard by uncontrolled gybes!

yacht heels when sailing because it feels as if it will tip over completely, especially when water is running over the side decks.

Dinghy sailors may be used to capsizing and do not really believe that a yacht is not going to do the same. Dinghies do not have ballast or a keel which is why they are so much less stable. If yachts were in danger of capsizing whenever there was a strong wind, yachting would not be the sport it is today. People certainly would not attempt to cross oceans, so have a little faith. In three years working with charters, we have never known anyone to capsize!

Perhaps you trust the yacht but not those sailing her. A yacht will often take care of itself. Excessive heel is usually the result of having too much sail up for the weather conditions, though sometimes freak gusts can cause an unexpected tilt. The more a yacht heels, the less of the rudder is left in the water, and eventually you will find yourself no longer able to steer. In most yachts the curve of the hull in the water then acts like a large rudder, and causes the yacht to turn into the direction of the wind, and come back upright with sails flapping.

Leeway

The main aim of the keel, as well as providing stability, is to prevent the sideways movement of the yacht through the water (leeway) that occurs particularly when the wind is forward of the beam. Some keel shapes are better at this than others which is why some yachts are able to sail in a direction much closer to the wind. For a yacht to sail well, the shape and angle of the sails must also be altered to suit the strength and direction of the wind.

Into the wind

No yacht is able to sail directly into the wind, however well designed. At a certain point, the sails will stall and start to flap. If you continue to turn towards the direction the wind is blowing from, the boat will eventually be head to wind.

Sailing with the wind coming almost over the bow is known as beating. Sailing close to the wind means heading as much towards the direction of the wind as is possible without stalling the sails. The limit is about 45 degrees to the wind, however well a yacht points. The closer a yacht is able to sail to the wind, the

THE CONTROLLED GYBE: Ensure no one is sitting or standing where they could be hit by the boom during the gybe. The coachroof is never a good place to sit when running downwind.

As the yacht turns, the working headsail sheet is released and the headsail is pulled in on the other side. The other side of the mainsail fills with wind, and the boom comes over as the mainsheet is let out in a controlled manner.

higher it is said to point. When beating, the sails are pulled in towards the centreline of the yacht which is then said to be close hauled. Most leeway is made on this point of sail.

Often you will be unable to sail in the direction you want to go because the wind is against you. This means that you will have to put in a series of tacks or zig-zags to make your way upwind. Altering course by putting the bow through the wind so the sails cross over to the other side is known as tacking *(see photos on pages 50-51).*

Across the wind

Reaching means sailing with the wind on the beam. Wind directly on the beam is known as a beam reach, just behind it a broad reach, and just in front of it a fine

The mainsheet is pulled in as far as possible towards the centreline before the stern passes through the eye of the wind. When everyone is ready the helmsman calls "Gybe-oh" and starts the turn.

The mainsheet traveller position may need to be changed from one side to the other. A controlled gybe like this should involve no bangs or jerks, but is progressively more difficult as the wind gets stronger.

or close reach. To set the sails, free them off until they just start to flap, after which pull them in again until the flapping stops.

With the wind

Running is sailing with the wind behind. The sails are let out to be as much at right angles as possible to the wind. A dead run is where the wind is directly behind.

The headsail will not fill properly because it is shielded by the mainsail, and can be taken to the other side – this is known as goosewinging.

When a yacht alters course so that its stern moves through the wind, causing the boom to cross from one side to the other, it is said to have gybed.

9 Boat Handling Under Sail

Sail trim is an easily learnt science at a basic level. Upwind performance is increased by the slot effect between sails.

SAIL TRIM

Most bareboat and flotilla yachts are chosen with both comfort and performance in mind, so fall into the cruiser/racer bracket. Sail trimming need not be over-complicated, though some yachts will have more things to tweak than others and some sailors will enjoy tweaking for its own sake.

Sail drive

The traditional Bermudian sloop had a large mainsail and a smaller headsail (jib), with the mainsail providing the majority of the driving force. Conversely most modern designs have a large headsail (genoa) and a smaller main, with a large area of overlap between the two. In this case it is the genoa that

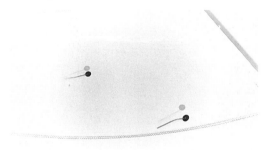

The 'telltales' clearly show how the air is flowing on both sides of the sail. If the sail is properly trimmed they should all be blowing backwards.

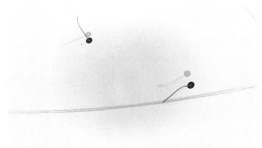

Here the upper telltale on the windward side is lifting, indicating that the sail must be pulled in, or the helmsman must bear away.

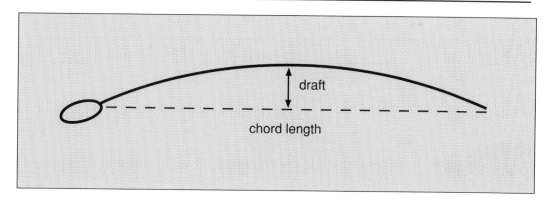

provides the greater drive, but equally as important is the relationship between the two, since performance is increased by what is known as the slot effect as wind passes between the overlapping sails. This is the complimentary effect the sails have on each other if positioned well, though some disagreement exists as to exactly how it works. Ideally the airflow comes off the leech of the genoa parallel to the surface of the mainsail, or it will either cause the mainsail to back, or cause the genoa to lose power. Viewed from behind, both sails should have the same shape and angle to the wind.

You need to adjust the sail trim for different wind strengths and sea states. For example, when beating in strong winds sheet the sails tight, whereas in lighter more variable winds, especially if there is any swell, loosening the sheets a little will pay dividends. Performance will also be improved by not trying to sail too close to the wind.

Sail shape

The distance between the luff and the leech of a sail is known as its chord length, and the draft is the depth of its curve. The degree and position of the deepest draft is important to aerodynamic performance. When sailing to windward, the maximum draft of the headsail should be about a third of the way back from the luff towards the leech, and halfway back on the mainsail. When reaching or running, the deepest draft on the headsail must come further back but never more than halfway. Draft position is changed by altering halyard and thereby luff tension. When beating, the stronger the wind the more the draft will tend to move aft, and therefore the more halyard tension is needed to counteract it. In light winds decrease halyard tension. When putting up a sail, tighten the halyard until a vertical crease appears near the luff. If this disappears when the sail fills with wind, the tension is OK. If not, loosen off the halyard until it does disappear. If there

are any bags or creases in the luff that look like washing on a line, the halyard is too slack. Do not alter the halyard tension of in-mast furling mainsails.

Positions of sheet fairleads will also affect the shape of a sail. For a sail to work well when beating, the curve should be uniform from top to bottom. If the fairlead for the foresail sheet is positioned correctly, all parts of the luff will start to back at the same time when you turn up to wind. When reefing the foresail, the fairleads must be moved forwards accordingly.

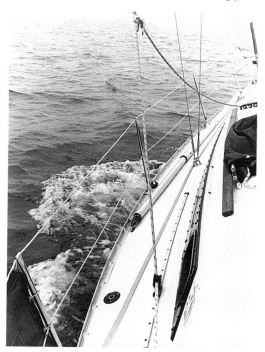

Sheeting angle is controlled by adjusting the sheet lead on its track. Moving the car forward tightens the leech and puts round in the foot. Moving it aft slackens the leech. The car will need to be adjusted whenever you change headsail or furl/unfurl it.

The mainsheet traveller allows the boom to be let out from the centreline, with the mainsheet still holding it down.

When the mainsail is let right out over the side of the boat, the mainsheet is unable to hold the boom down.

Vibration

Sometimes the leech of a sail will start to vibrate when beating. Try tightening the leech line to correct it. If this does nothing but cause a hook in the leech, it may be that the sheet fairlead is too far back. But be careful when moving the fairlead forward to loosen the leech line first, and don't put too much tension on the leech or it will stretch.

Boom angle

The angle of the boom to the centreline is controlled by the mainsheet, and by the kicking strap or boom vang. When beating, the mainsheet holds the boom down as well as holding it in towards the centreline of the boat. A mainsheet traveller allows the boom to be let out, but the sheet to continue to hold it down. When reaching or running the mainsheet is no longer able to hold the boom down, and the sail will start to twist and spill out wind from the top. The task of holding down the boom to prevent this must now pass to the kicking strap (vang).

A twist in the sail reduces performance because the upper part of the sail is no longer driving as it should be. When running, twist creates an unwanted force at the top of the mast which can cause a rolling motion, particularly in strong winds, making it important to maintain kicking strap tension.

Furthermore, if the boom is allowed to move up and down with the action of the waves, sail shape is continually disturbed, with resulting loss of drive.

Using sail twist

When reaching or beating in stronger winds, allowing the sail to twist can sometimes be advantageous. When reaching, spilling wind from the top of the sail by loosening the kicker (vang) will reduce heel and associated weather helm (tendency of the bow to try and point up into wind). When beating, twist can be achieved by moving the mainsheet traveller a bit higher (further to windward) and loosening off the mainsheet slightly. This can be useful when winds are not strong or constant enough to demand a reef.

Backstay adjustment

Many yachts have the facility to alter the tension of the backstay, and thereby the shape of the mast. Tensioning the backstay causes the mast top to bend backwards and the centre to bow forwards, and therefore affects the shape of the sails and tension on the forestay. As a rough guide, when sailing downwind tension is decreased, and when sailing to windward tension is increased to take out slack in the forestay and flatten the mainsail. The lighter the wind, the less backstay is needed when beating.

The task of holding the boom down passes to the vang or kicking strap, which prevents it lifting in the air.

DOWNWIND

When running (with the wind) the wind may feel much less than it really is because your motion reduces it. For example, if you were doing 6 knots downwind in a 10 knot breeze, you would only 'feel' four knots of wind. But beware: when you turn up towards the wind you will be hit by the full force of the breeze - plus your 'motion wind'.

When running directly downwind, keeping both mainsail and genoa full at the same time and continually watching that the mainsail does not gybe can make for frustrating and stressful sailing, especially if there is a rolling sea trying to push you off course. It may be worth altering course and making it less of a dead run, or continuing under main or genoa alone. Some yachts will have a thin wisker pole with which to hold out the genoa on the opposite side to the mainsail, from the clew to a point on the mast. If not, a spinnaker pole will do just as well, but do not be tempted to use a boathook because if it were to break (which is quite possible) it could spear the unfortunate person holding it.

Gybe preventers

When travelling longer distances on a dead run, some find it preferable to rig a system to prevent accidental and therefore uncontrolled gybes, though no less care must be taken to steer a good course. A gybe preventer is a length of line used to pull the boom forward to its position near the shrouds. If the sail is allowed to fill with wind from the other side, the boat will stop in the water and you will be unable to steer. It is therefore essential to be able to release the preventer immediately. To rig a preventer, tie a long piece of line to the end of the boom and take it forward to the bow, through a cleat and back again to the cockpit where it can be cleated off without a knot in the end. Try to make sure that the line is long enough so that, when released, the boom can swing over to the other side.

Sailing downwind is fine on a calm and steady day, but can demand skill and good nerves if the wind is blowing hard. The location here is Thailand.

10 Setting the Sails

The cruising chute is a modern addition to the sail wardrobe which increases downwind performance.

Getting sails ready for use will usually be much easier at a mooring than away from it, so it is a good idea to do as much as you can before setting off. If any of the sails are roller-furling, check that the furling lines and sheets are ready to use, and that no other lines are tangled - such as a spare halyard caught up in the furling system at the top of the mast. Sorting out knitting is much easier when the deck is not moving about.

Headsail selection

You may find a selection of headsails on racing boats,

traditional designs, some crewed charters, adventure charters, and those used by sailing schools. The sails are given different names depending on their size and type, such as genoa (large) and jib (small).

If you have a selection of headsails find out which one will be suitable for the weather conditions, and get it in position on deck with the halyard attached to the head, or easily to hand if it cannot be kept taut until used. Attach the sheets to the clew. If the sail is attached to the forestay by clasps known as hanks, clip them on ready. Fix the tack to the appropriate point at the bottom of the forestay. There will probably be

To raise the mainsail, attach the halyard, making sure it is not caught round the spreaders. Remove all the sail ties prior to hoisting.

Pull on the halyard, making sure the luff of the sail does not jam. The halyard should be taken round a winch as soon as there is any tension.

some means of securing the sail to the safety rails until it is ready to be used, such as pieces of stretchy rope known as shock-cord. Make sure the sheets are not on the wrong side of the shrouds or safety rails, and run through the fairleads correctly. Check there are stopper knots in the ends.

Sail protection

Sails left in position ready to use each day, such as the mainsail or roller-furling genoa, will have some form of protection from the elements, most notably ultra violet light from the sun. The exposed edge of a rolled sail will usually have a sewn-on layer known as a sunstrip, and a cover will usually be provided for the mainsail. Always put the cover on after mooring up at the end of the day, and take it off before leaving so the sail is ready for use.

Mainsail hoist

Attach the halyard to the head, and take up the slack, so that the halyard doesn't become caught anywhere such as around the spreaders on the mast. Loosen the kicking strap (vang) and set the topping lift so that the boom is roughly at right angles to the mast. If a reef is likely to be needed, now is the time to put it in.

Hoisting a sail is much easier when the boat is pointing into the wind, or at least with the sheet let off so that the sail is flapping. If the sail is allowed to fill with wind it will be difficult and sometimes impossible to hoist.

To hoist the mainsail, take off the sail ties and put them somewhere safe. Pull on the halyard either from at the mast or in the cockpit, depending on where the end leads to. It is important to watch the sail as it goes up to make sure it is not getting caught.

The edge of the sail known as the luff may be attached to the mast in a number of ways. Sometimes

it will need to be fed inside a groove as it goes up, and may require supervision by someone at the mast to make sure it feeds in correctly. Sometimes the luff will have runners attached that are fed into a groove instead. These will usually be left in the groove, though may be taken out when the sail is reefed, and should therefore be checked to make sure they are in place before hoisting. Some will have cars that are permanently fixed on a track on the mast.

It may be necessary to use a winch to achieve the desired tension on the mainsail halyard. *Sweating* the halyard at the mast can also help. One hand pulls the line as it comes from the top of the mast to the cleat or block at the bottom, and the other hand then quickly pulls in the slack from the other side of the cleat or block as the first hand releases it. You will need less tension on the halyard in light winds, so check with the skipper how tight it should be.

If the sail is very difficult to hoist, make sure there is no tension on the mainsheet or kicking strap(vang). When the sail is fully hoisted, let off any tension on the topping lift so the boom is supported by the sail, set the kicker(vang) and mainsheet traveller car, and pull in on the mainsheet as required for the desired course.

Headsail hoist

A non-furling headsail is hoisted in much the same way, the luff being attached to the forestay either in a groove or with hanks. There may be a system at the bottom of the forestay which holds the luff in the correct position to help it feed into the groove easily. Sometimes there will be a twin groove to allow another sail to be hoisted before taking the old one down: this prevents the boat losing speed when racing. As long as there is no tension on the sheets, there is no need to turn up directly into the wind to

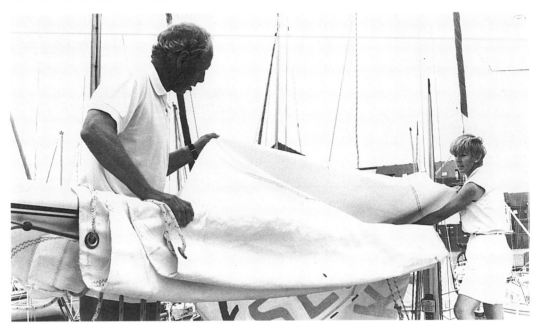

When dropping the mainsail fold it on top of the boom, putting sail ties on as you go.

hoist the headsail.

It is usually easier to hoist the mainsail before the headsail, as the mainsail can usually be kept from flapping by pulling in hard on the mainsheet even with the boat pointing into the wind. If the headsail is hoisted or unfurled first, it is more at risk of being damaged as it flaps about before being set. Many people hoist a mainsail even when motoring into the wind as it helps provide stability in the waves and gives a more comfortable ride. But try to avoid letting the main flap.

Dropping sails

When taking the sails down before mooring, the usual procedure is to turn on the engine, furl or take down the headsail, and then lower the main. To lower the headsail, let off the tension on the sheet so that the sail flaps, then let off the halyard. Make sure it does not tangle or jam on the way and that you do not loose the end. Someone will need to be at the bow to collect in the sail as it comes down. Pull only on the luff (to avoid stretching or damage), and if the yacht is pointing towards the wind the sail should fall onto the deck, though it may need a helping hand to prevent any flopping over the side. The sail can either be put into its bag, or tied back onto the safety rails and put away later. Take up any slack on the sheets back in the cockpit, and make sure the end of the halyard is secured.

To lower the mainsail, first make sure there is sufficient tension on the topping lift to support the boom as the sail comes down. With the boat pointing into the wind, let off the mainsheet and then the halyard. (Laying out the halyard in loose coils beforehand will help it to run smoothly.) It may be necessary to help the sail down by pulling on the luff.

Once the sail is down, pull in the mainsheet to stop the boom swinging while the crew fold the sail. Some sails will fall fairly neatly in folds on top of the boom, though others will need more help. If the luff remains attached to the mast, one person can fold it from the end nearest the cockpit and put ties on as they go. If the luff detaches from the mast you will need a person at both ends to lay the sail in folds on top of the boom. If folding the sail proves difficult under way, or you are short-handed, wrapping it up inside itself and tying it temporarily will suffice until you are safely moored up.

Some yachts are fitted with a system that allows for easier handling of the mainsail. They have a fully battened mainsail (the battens run horizontally all the way from the luff to the leech), *lazy jacks*, and cars on the luff fixed permanently to a track on the mast. Lazy jacks are lines that run from boom to mast either side of the sail, which catch the sail between them as it comes down. The battens help the sail to fold as it does so, and the runners keep the luff in place on the mast. This system is becoming increasingly popular on cruising yachts, especially if the mainsail area is

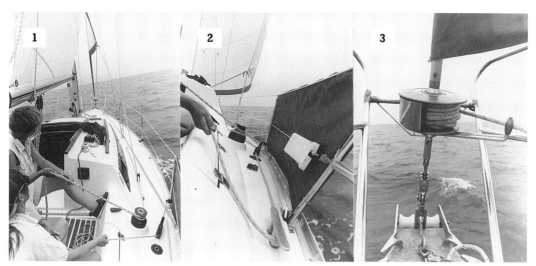

Headsail roller-furling is completely controlled from the cockpit. There is no need to go on the foredeck. 1. You can unroll as much of the sail as you require. 2. However roller-furling headsails are at their most efficient when they are fully unrolled. 3. The furling line is wound round the rotating drum, and must be kept under tension.

large and unmanageable for a short-handed crew.

ROLLER FURLING
Headsail roller furling

The majority of bareboat and flotilla yachts are now fitted with roller furling genoas. The sail remains permanently hoisted, and is rolled around the forestay. To unfurl the sail, coil the furling line to make sure there are no knots, and pay it out. At the same time pull on one of the sheets and allow the wind to fill the sail. If it is at all windy, there may be considerable tension on the furling line, and it is advisable to take a turn around a winch or cleat to prevent it pulling through your hands. The furling line winds around a drum at the bottom of the forestay. Keeping tension on the furling line will prevent riding turns on the drum, which will be difficult to remove when it comes to rolling in the sail.

To furl the sail, let off the tension on the sheet, and pull in on the furling line. As long as the sheet is loose, it should be possible to furl the sail fairly easily. If the wind is strong it may be more difficult and you may need to use a winch, but it is very important to make sure there is no other reason for the line being tight, such as its jamming on the drum or some foul-up at the top of the mast. When the sail is furled, cleat off the furling line, then tension and cleat the sheets.

The disadvantages of roller furling headsails

Despite their advantages, some sailors have

reservations about roller furling headsails. The first area of concern is sailing performance. It is not possible to change to a heavier or lighter sail as conditions demand (unless you have two which is unlikely), and the shape of the reefed sail (half rolled) is often not as good as a purpose-built sail. However, unless you are racing seriously the last ounce of speed is not critical.

The second problem is the possibility of the system jamming. This is often caused by a spare line such as the spinnaker halyard becoming wrapped around the furling system at the top of the forestay as the sail is rolled in or out. The rogue line then jams and prevents the sail from being rolled back the other way. To prevent this happening, keep any spare halyards pulled back out of the way and tightly cleated off. It is easy to see from the bottom of the mast if the system is clear before you go out each day. If you do get a wrapped halyard, take the end and unwrap it from around the forestay. Attempting to roll in the sail by pulling on the furling line will only make the situation worse, and could even pull the forestay down if excessive force is used.

The other reason for jamming is that the furling line becomes fouled in the drum at the bottom of the forestay. The only solution will be to go up on deck and undo the turns by hand. Riding turns are able to form if the line is allowed to turn loosely on the drum, so avoid them by keeping tension on the reefing line as you unfurl the sail and keep the end tensioned and cleated off once the sail is fully unfurled.

Above and right: To slab reef the mainsail, release halyard tension, pull down the luff, and attach a reefing cringle to the hook on the boom by the mast. If there are 'cars' holding the luff of the sail to the mast track, it may be necessary to drop some of them out of the track. Re-tension the main halyard, and then pull down hard on the appropriate reefing line with the boom vang and mainsheet let right off. The pulled-down flap of the sail can be folded or tied out of the way.

Close-up of a mainsail furled inside a mast. The control lines are all taken back to the cockpit.

Thirdly, strong winds can make furling the sail more difficult. Make sure the sheets are loose and the sail flapping, before winding in the furling line using a winch. If you get huge resistance, check that the system is free before using any more force. If jamming does occur, and you are unable to sort it out and the wind is too strong to allow you to roll the sail away by hand, as a last resort roll the sail by removing both sheets from the clew and turning the boat around in circles. Be careful on the foredeck or you may be hit by the sail as it whips about. When it is finally furled, re-attach the sheets and tie the sail in place on the forestay.

Mainsail roller furling

Some yachts have systems for roller furling the mainsail. Earlier designs use a rolling boom which is turned by a handle, rolling the mainsail on itself as it goes. Newer designs roll the sail inside either the mast or the boom. If the sail is rolled onto or inside the boom, the halyard is released and the sail taken down as it is rolled. If the sail is rolled into the mast, the sail is permanently hoisted and attached to the boom only at the clew, and is therefore known as loose footed.

In-mast furling systems use two furling lines, one to pull the sail out and the other to pull it in. The halyard must be kept tight, so be careful not to inadvertently release it from its cleat. To unfurl the sail, use the topping lift to hold the boom at right angles to the mast, loosen the mainsheet and point the boat head-to-wind. The unfurling line is pulled out, and the furling line paid in. If the furling line is not controlled as

it goes in, it may become jammed inside the mast. Cleat off both lines when the sail is unfurled and if necessary use a winch to make sure the clew is correctly positioned on the boom. When furling in the sail, again keep hold of both lines and pay one out as you pull the other one in. Watch the sail to make sure it is rolling properly and not folding at all on its way in. If you need to use the winch such as in strong winds, first make sure there is no jamming and that you are head to wind. Keep tension on the unfurling line to stop the main flapping and damaging the clew car.

The disadvantages of a roller furling mainsail

Roller furling mainsails can jam. When using an in-mast system keep tension on both the furling and unfurling lines. Prevent the sail folding on its way into the mast by making sure the halyard tension is good and that the boom is at 90 degrees to the mast. (The halyard will normally be tensioned and secured already, and should only be adjusted if it appears to be loose with wrinkles in the luff.)

With in-boom furling, make sure the boom is at 90 degrees to the mast when furling. Watch the sail as it is rolled away to make sure there is no folding, and if it starts to do so stop and pull it out again. If the sail is difficult to furl or unfurl, make sure you are head-to-wind and that the sheet is loose. If for some reason you are unable to roll the sail away, it is still possible to take it down by releasing the halyard in the conventional way.

REEFING

To reef a headsail either partially roll it, or change to a smaller one. To reef the mainsail either roll it or use the slab-reefing. Here a flap of sail is taken down, creating a new foot which is then secured to the top of the boom. First let off the halyard tension sufficiently so the crew can pull down the luff and attach the reefing cringle (reinforced hole) on the sail to the reefing hook on the boom. Then take up the halyard tension again. Finally, wind in the reefing line to pull the new clew of the mainsail to the aft end of the boom. Sometimes the reefing line is led back to the cockpit, and sometimes to a winch at the mast.

Reefing lines will often be of different colours to help you determine which one you should be pulling, as there will usually be two or three options as to how small you want to make the sail. Use reefing ties to hold the unused flap of sail to the underside of the boom. You can often let off the mainsheet and reef the mainsail while keeping the foresail drawing alone.

To release a reef, first undo the ties, then release the kicker (vang) and the reefing line. Slacken the halyard so the crew can unhook the cringle. Finally tension the halyard and kicker. It is important to do it in this order to prevent damage to the sail.

Some systems allow for easier reefing by using one line to secure both luff and leech to the boom. The halyard tension is let off and this one line tensioned to reef the sail, after which the halyard is tensioned again. Not surprisingly this is known as one-line reefing. The magic line is usually led to the cockpit.

When to reef sails

Deciding when to reef the sails, by how much and in what order, will depend on the strength and direction of the wind and on the type of yacht. Determining the best sail configuration is largely a matter of experimentation, but in general the rule is to reef early. The last thing you want is to be struggling on deck with a problem in a stronger wind than you would like. If you have the option to change foresails, it is important not to risk damage by using too light a sail for the wind conditions.

Heeling over

If you are sailing with the wind forward of the beam, reef if heel is excessive. Otherwise, the boat will make leeway, and also suffer weather helm, with the bow constantly trying to point up into the wind. If you are overpowered you will either have to keep spilling

The reefing lines pull down the leech of the sail to the end of the boom. There may be as many as three lines to give three depths of reef. These are usually colour-coded and are led back to the cockpit.

Before using the cruising chute, check there are no tangled lines inside the snuffer. Attach the tack at the bottom of the forestay. Attach the sheet to the clew .

wind from the mainsail by releasing the sheet, or turning the boat frequently up into the wind (luffing). Reducing sail area will cause no loss of speed, allow you to keep a better course, and give a more comfortable ride. All in all there is no advantage to keeping a boat on its side.

Which sail first?

Many sailors reef the foresail first. This prevents backing of the mainsail as wind leaves the genoa, and decreases the amount of sail area aft of the mast which should help reduce weather helm. With a roller reefing genoa, it is easy to take in a bit of sail and see if things improve. If not, put a reef in the mainsail.

It is important to have the sails balanced for the yacht to handle well. If you are about to leave a mooring and think you might need to reef, put one in the mainsail before you go out, because it will be easier to shake out the reef if you do not need it than put it in if you do.

Wind-watch

Watch out for wind such as when a squall passes over. Dark ominous clouds coming your way and wind on the water are indications that it is time to reduce sail. Be prepared to ease sheets in the gusts, or you could find yourself heeling severely.

Stronger winds and gusts sometimes occur when there are cliffs or mountains upwind of you. These are known as catabatic winds and their effects can be seen on the water below.

When you have hoisted the cruising chute inside the snuffer, make sure the snuffer is free by pulling it up a little way and then back down. Next take it halfway and then back down. If all is well you can then pull it up all the way and allow the chute to fill. In this way you can be sure there will be no problem pulling it down.

CRUISING CHUTES AND SPINNAKERS

Cruising chutes, drifters, gennakers and spinnakers are large balloon-shaped sails that are flown from the front of a boat and used for downwind sailing. Some are essentially a large genoa, others such as the spinnaker use a pole or poles to help hold them in position.

A spinnaker can give exciting sailing when running or reaching, and need not be dangerous in experienced or well organised hands, but can cause serious problems for the ill-prepared. Many companies do not provide spinnakers due to the problems they can cause. As an alternative, a smaller and less demanding sail such as a cruising chute is fairly easy to use, making it a popular option on many charter yachts. This type of sail is often advertised as a downwind cruising sail.

A cruising chute is rather like a large lightweight genoa, but the luff is only attached to the forestay at

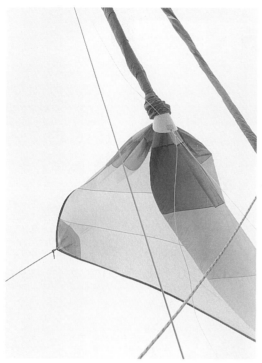

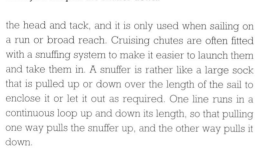

To snuff the cruising chute, first spill some wind by easing the sheet or turning the yacht more off the wind. Then you can pull the snuffer down.

Pull the snuffer all the way down. When not in use, pack the cruising chute away into its bag.

the head and tack, and it is only used when sailing on a run or broad reach. Cruising chutes are often fitted with a snuffing system to make it easier to launch them and take them in. A snuffer is rather like a large sock that is pulled up or down over the length of the sail to enclose it or let it out as required. One line runs in a continuous loop up and down its length, so that pulling one way pulls the snuffer up, and the other way pulls it down.

Hoisting a cruising chute

Before using the sail, check that there is no tangling of any of the lines or sail inside the snuffer. Attach the tack to a point at the bottom of the forestay, a sheet to the clew, then hoist the sail to the top of the forestay with the spinnaker halyard, and with the snuffer down. Ideally keep one side of the snuffing loop on the windward side of the sail and the other to leeward.

To fly the sail, first make sure the snuffer is free by pulling it up a little way and then back down. Next take it up halfway and then back down. In this way you can be sure there will be no problem when it comes to putting the sail away. Finally take the snuffer to the top, allow the sail to fill and adjust the sheet.

To snuff the sail, spill some wind by loosening the sheet or turning the boat towards the wind. Then simply pull down the snuffer until it completely covers the cruising chute once again.

To gybe a cruising chute, shift it and take the sheet over to the other side before flying the sail again.

11 Winching

Without some form of assistance, handling the lines on a sailing yacht would demand superhuman strength. Before you take up body-building or cancel your holiday, the good news is that help is at hand in the form of mechanical and sometimes electrical aids.

Systems of pulleys (blocks) are used to give extra purchase on a rope such as the mainsheet, mainsheet traveller and kicker (vang). The more times a rope runs backwards and forwards through the pulleys, the more power you have. The anchor can be raised by putting turns of the anchor line on the drum of a windlass, which is turned by a lever inserted in the side.

The advent of the winch

In the early days of racing large yachts, it was not unheard of for the entire crew to be made up of rugby players. Equipment has improved since then and winches are one of the devices making sail handling much easier and quicker. Winches are usually found in the cockpit for genoa sheets and spinnaker sheets and guys, and on the coachroof or mast for halyards and reefing lines.

A winch gives holding power due to friction between the rope and the drum. The more turns of rope you have, the greater the holding power. If the rope starts to slip, use another turn. The drum will only rotate one way, so a rope can be pulled in and then held by the drum, which is unable to turn back the other way.

Pulling power is increased in two ways, firstly by leverage and secondly by a system of gears. Simple 'single-stage' winches make use of a handle to give leverage: the longer the handle the easier it is to wind. A 'two-stage' winch will be easier to turn one way than the other. When the effort of turning it one way becomes too much, use the other direction to finish off. The line won't come in as fast but the job will be a lot easier. There may even be more stages available, activated perhaps by a push button on top of the winch. The effect is rather like changing gear on a bicycle for more power going up a hill.

Make sure you know how all the winches work and their uses before you set off on a flotilla. They are there to make your job easy, but treat them with respect.

Winch handles

The winch handle is removable and frequently lives in a pocket in the cockpit so it is conveniently to hand when needed. Some simply fit in to the top of the winch rather like a nut in the end of a spanner, and others are locked in place using a small lever on the top of the handle, which must be used to attach and detach the handle.

Make sure the handle is properly in place so as not to damage the splines where it connects with the winch. Most winch handles will sink if thrown over the side, so be careful where you leave them, especially the non-locking kind.

Self-tailing

A self-tailing winch grips the end of the line so you have both hands free to turn the handle. Put a few turns on the winch and then lead the end of the line around the part at the top that provides the grip. As you turn the winch, the line is automatically fed through and held fast by this grip.

Using a winch

To use a winch spin it to see which way you should load the rope, and put a few turns of rope on. It is important to keep tension on the line when pulling in to stop turns becoming trapped one beneath the other, known as *riding turns*. You may find it easier to start with only one or two turns on the winch when pulling in long lengths of slack line, such as when tacking and pulling in the genoa sheet. As the line tightens, put another turn on and attach the winch handle to wind in the rest. This is easier with two people as one tails (pulls on the end of the line) and the other grind (turns the winch). One person can do both, though it is a bit slower.

Be careful to keep your hands out of the way or they will be trapped between rope and drum To let out some of the line from around a winch, use the flat palm of your hand to ease it out slowly. To release a line under tension, such as when releasing the genoa sheet at the beginning of a turn, pull the loose end swiftly in an upwards direction until all the line is free, and then let go.

Riding turns

If you do end up with a riding turn, do something about it as quickly as possible, because it will simply become worse and more difficult to release the more the winch is turned or the more tension is applied. First you will need to take the tension off the line. One way is to attach another line with a rolling hitch and take up the strain on it using another winch, which leaves you free to release the riding turn.

Left: Winching is easier with two people. The crew on the left 'tails' by pulling in the rope as the crew on the right winds the winch. With a self-tailing winch one crew can perform both roles.
Below left: Be very careful not to trap your hands between the rope and the drum. To let out some rope, use the palm of your hand to ease the turns round.
Below right: To release a rope under tension, pull the loose end swiftly upwards until all the rope is free, and then let go.

An electric anchor winch makes the job easy on a large yacht where there is a very large weight of chain. The control buttons are in the foreground.

Anchor winches

Size of ground tackle usually determines whether or not a yacht is fitted with a bow anchor winch, though smaller yachts can have them. Some are purely mechanical and consist of a free-moving drum over which the anchor line is run. If it is designed for chain, there will be a groove which grips the links as they go round. The drum can be turned with a lever to pull the line in. Turning it the other way operates a brake. This is useful when controlling how fast the anchor line is let out when dropping the bow anchor. The drum turns freely to let the line out, and stops as the brake takes hold. Use the brake gently or it can jam due to the force of the chain rattling out against it.

Winding the line in bit by bit can be a little slow, and it may sometimes be easier to pull it in by hand. Electrically operated winches are quicker though not always easier. The electric motor can only be used if there is sufficient power, which usually means having the engine running with fairly fast revs though it does not have to be in gear. If the engine revs are too slow, the electrical circuit may 'trip out' and need resetting before it can be used again. Make sure you know what engine speed is required, and where to reset the trip should it be necessary.

Electric winch overload

Overloading a winch, such as when trying to use it to pull up the entire anchor and chain from 20 metres of water in a strong wind all in one go, may also cause it to trip, blow a fuse or even burn out the electrics. In situations such as these, to prevent overloading use the engine to drive in the direction of the anchor, and lift it in stages. If the winch cannot cope or breaks down, you may have the facility to wind the line in manually with a handle. If not, attach a piece of line to the chain at the bow and take it back to a winch in the cockpit. Winch in the line until you come to the chain. Cleat off the chain, remove the line, and reattach it to the chain at the bow. You can pull up the entire chain this way if necessary. Make sure you pile it back inside the anchor locker with the end nearest the anchor finishing on top, or it will be difficult to get out again next time.

12 Knots, Lines and Fenders

KNOTS

If the only knots you are familiar with are the granny and shoelace bow, don't worry, you do not need to know every knot that has ever been tied to be a competent sailor. We have sailed thousands of miles on three knots – the bowline, round turn and two half hitches and stopper knot without ever having to resort to the monkey's fist, sheepshank or truck driver's half hitch, however useful or more appropriate they would have been. Stick to a few common but versatile knots that you can guarantee to get by on, and when they are second nature try a few more.

Clove hitch

Useful for securing a fender to a rail.

Round turn and two half hitches

Good for securing a mooring line to a ring or post, and a good alternative for securing fenders.

Bowline

Used to form an eye on the end of a rope, such as when attaching a sheet to the foresail.

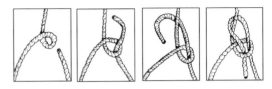

Stopper knot

Used at the end of a sheet to prevent it running through a block, or on the end of a halyard to prevent losing it inside the mast.

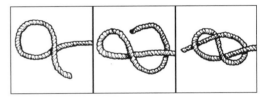

Sheet bend

For joining two ropes together, particularly of different thickness. A double sheet bend is extra secure.

Right: The double sheet bend gives extra security.

The cam cleat is often used to lock the mainsheet on a small yacht. To release the sheet, pull it towards you and down from the jaws of the cleat in one movement.

Shackles

An alternative to the knot is the shackle. Shackles come in all shapes and sizes and will be seen serving a variety of purposes throughout any yacht. Sometimes a line will have a shackle attached to the end to enable it to be secured quickly without having to spend time tying a knot, such as on the end of a halyard where it attaches to the top of a sail. Here you may find a snap shackle, which is particularly useful, being easily opened and closed, and having no loose moving parts to drop at the wrong moment.

ROPES AND LINES
Care and use of ropes

A well-coiled rope, neatly stowed, will be of far more use when you need it than a tangled heap of line lurking in the cockpit locker; and the end of a halyard, coiled and secured to the foot of the mast will be far less likely to find its way overboard and around your propeller than one casually left on deck.

Coiling a rope

1. To coil a rope, one hand and arm stays still and holding the coils, while the other does the coiling. With the still hand, take hold of one end, and if the rope is fixed to something at one end, make sure it is the fixed end you take hold of.

2. With the other hand, take an arm's length of rope, coil it round, and pass it into the still hand. A twist with the wrist of the coiling hand will help to take out any kinks or twists as you go along, which helps the coils to lie flat.

3. Repeat until you've coiled the whole rope. The free end of the rope can now be used to fasten the coils together, so wrap it around the coils two or three times, working from the bottom upwards, and then push a loop of rope through the hole you will have made in the top of the coils. Open the loop, fold it back over the coils, and pull the free end to secure it.

Two basic staghorn cleats being used for mooring ropes. In this case the port and starboard ropes are looped over the cleats using bowlines, passed round rings in the dock, and then taken back to the cleats to be tied off.

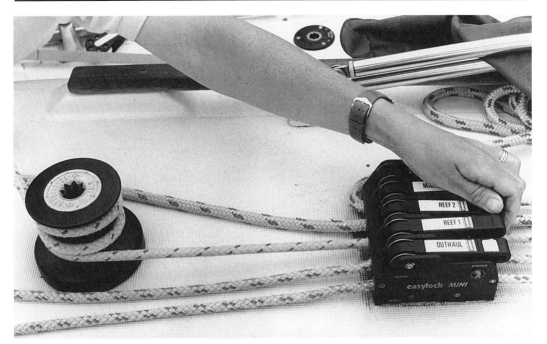

The clutch/lever arm cleat is a sophisticated newcomer. It enables you to wind the line in with the lever locked in the down position, or to unload the line immediately by lifting the lever.

Securing a rope to a boat

Every yacht has points on deck at which ropes or lines can be secured. Most are designed and placed with specific functions in mind, such as staghorn cleats on the mast for securing halyards or the topping lift; staghorn cleats on the bow for the anchor line or mooring lines; and lever arm cleats on the coachroof for securing lines that come back to the cockpit from the mast.

Basic cleat/staghorn cleat

1. Take hold of the line towards the fixed end and wrap it once around the base of the cleat.
2. Criss-cross the line over the horns in a figure-of-eight, at least two or three times.
3. Finish with a final turn around the cleat.

The more criss-crosses you make, the more secure the line will be, and by finishing with the free end of the line, you will be able to undo it easily, even if the fixed end is under considerable strain.

Jamming cleat

Often found near a winch in the cockpit, and designed to secure a line such as a genoa sheet once the main strain has been taken by the winch. A single turn will jam behind the cleat, and is just as easily released.

Cam cleat

Used to secure the mainsheet on small knots.

1. Pull the line through the cleat. The action of the jaws will hold it secure.
2. Release by pulling the line upwards to free it from between the jaws.

Clutch/lever arm cleat

Often used for halyards and sometimes for reefing lines on the side of the boom or mast.

1. Pull the line as taut as required and depress the lever to secure. It is also possible to pull the line through with the arm in the depressed position which can help with final tensioning.
2. To release, take up the tension on the line, and raise the lever. If the tension is too great, use a winch to wind in the line, hold it, and then raise the lever.

Be careful not to trap another boat's line under your line on a bollard. Always pass your line underneath.

Mooring lines

Probably the best knot to use on the shore end of your line is a round turn and two half hitches, which can be easily undone under tension. Some mooring lines have a permanent loop in the end, created by splicing the end back on itself, which is designed to be slipped over a bollard, post or cleat. This can create more room on a cleat if it needs to accommodate more than one line. In the same way some people like to secure a line using a loop formed by a bowline. Whatever you use, make sure that at least one end of the line can be undone when under load.

Leading back and courtesy

Sometimes if a ring is taken up with several other ropes, it may be easier to secure one end of the line to the yacht, pass it through the ring, and tie the other end back on board. Be careful not to trap another boat's line under your line on a bollard: they may have to resort to releasing your line in order to free their own. If you tie a round turn and two half hitches, tie it beneath their line, and if you use a loop pass it up inside their loop before putting it over the bollard so neither of you will be inconvenienced.

Make sure any lengths of line left over are coiled and out of the way on deck.

Stowing lines

Once you have left a mooring and safely negotiated your way out of the harbour or marina, take in all the mooring lines, coil them and stow them in a locker. Do not leave any on deck while underway even if they are tied on and coiled, as they could still be lost overboard.

Halyards

Halyards are used to raise and lower sails. One end attaches to the top of the sail, usually by means of a shackle, and when not in use can be detached and clipped near the bottom of the mast to be close at hand when required. The other end passes up the mast to a pulley at or near the top, and then down again either internally or externally, where it is cleated at the bottom or led back to the cockpit via pulleys. Sometimes part of the halyard, at the end which attaches to the top of the sail, will be made of wire, and the other end of rope.

Tidying halyards

When a sail is raised, the amount of loose halyard at deck level increases considerably. If cleated at the mast, coil the halyard and attach it to the cleat by reaching your spare hand through the middle of the coils and taking hold of the line as it comes from the cleat. Pull a loop through the centre and twist it to form a small loop which can then be slipped over the top horn of the cleat.

Unless specific stowage such as a clip or bag is

Pull a loop through the centre of the halyard coil, and
twist to form a small loop on top.

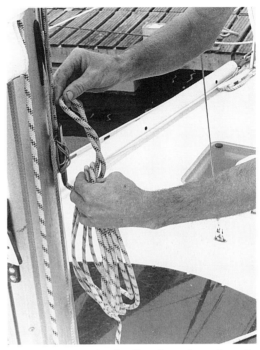

The small loop can then be slipped over the top horn of
the cleat to hold the coil.

In the case of a foresail or headsail, the two sheets are
often attached directly to the clew with a bowline. Using
a shackle can be dangerous, since it may hit someone
when the sail is flapping.

A typical mainsheet arrangement on a small yacht. One
problem here is that the mainsheet and its traveller
obstruct the companionway, which means some care
must be taken when passing.

Although some yachts have a locker to stow the stern anchor, many do not have this facility. This is one method of keeping the anchor, chain and warp on the pushpit.

provided, halyards led back to the cockpit can be coiled and laid over a winch near the cleat. Some sailors like to throw the loose ends down inside the companionway, but if you do, be careful not to trip anyone up.

Sheets

The sheet is the main control line of a sail. One end of the sheet is attached to the sail. In the case of a foresail this is often attached directly with a knot such as a bowline. The mainsail sheet (mainsheet) is attached indirectly to the underside of the boom via a system of pulleys known as blocks which give added purchase on the line. A cam cleat incorporated into the last pulley allows the sheet to be held in position and released easily when required.

The other end of a foresail sheet is led back to the cockpit via fairleads and a pulley. From here it can be pulled in and cleated with the aid of a winch. Keep the end free of tangles and coiled out of the way. Stopper

knots in the ends of main and foresail sheets are a wise precaution against losing them through the pulleys and out over the side where they can flail out of reach in the wind, and cause you to lose control of the sail completely.

Anchor lines

The usual means of attaching an anchor are chain, rope or a combination of the two. Sometimes only the section nearest the anchor will be chain, and the remainder rope (also known as warp). The combination of anchor, chain and warp is commonly called 'ground tackle'.

Most yachts will have at least two anchors, one at the bow and one at the stern. In Britain the stern anchor is usually smaller and normally used as a spare, often being referred to as the *kedge* or second anchor. In parts of the Mediterranean it is very common to use an anchor from the stern to hold a yacht in a bows-to position to a quay.

Most yachts have a locker on the bow in which to stow the anchor and line. There will normally be a point in the bottom to which to tie the end so that it will never be lost overboard. For added security, always tie the line to a cleat on deck before letting go the anchor. A common mistake is to have the end of the line that comes from the anchor at the top of the cleat instead of at the bottom, which makes it impossible to release under load.

Stowing the anchor line

To stow the anchor line at the bow, flake it carefully back into the locker, undoing any twists as you go to prevent tangling next time. Finish with the anchor laid on top.

Although some yachts have a locker to stow the stern anchor line, many do not. You may find you have to flake it into a bucket tied onto the stern, or to coil and secure it to the anchor which is hooked onto a bracket on the stern rail.

Roller reefing lines

Many modern charter yachts are fitted with systems for roller-furling the sails. Roller-furling foresails are extremely common, with the sail remaining permanently hoisted, and stowed or made smaller *(reefed)* by wrapping it around the forestay, similar to a roller blind. Some mainsails are also furled by rolling, such as inside the mast. Both systems involve the use of furling lines, usually led back to the cockpit for ease of use with strategically placed cleats to secure them.

The more fenders you use the better. They should be concentrated round the wide part of the yacht, at the right height.

Topping lift, kicking strap (boom vang) and reefing lines

The topping lift supports the boom when not in use. The kicking strap helps to control the horizontal angle of the boom and thereby adds to the control of the shape of the mainsail. Reefing lines are used when reducing the mainsail area when the strength of the wind demands it.

Protecting lines

Most modern synthetic ropes are fairly hard wearing but will be damaged by rubbing on sharp corners. Lead mooring lines through the fairleads at bow and stern, and pad the rope with a piece of old rag or plastic bag if it is rubbing on the edge of the quay.

When a rope is divided into lengths, the cut ends are sealed to prevent the strands unravelling. Many, though not all, can be sealed with heat which adds no bulk to the cut end. Sometimes the strands will come undone and it is important that the end is re-sealed as soon as possible, because left to its own devices it will rapidly unravel and soon become totally useless. As a first resort and temporary measure, tie a knot in the end of the line to prevent it getting any worse. A knot is prone to getting caught, so aim to carry out a more

permanent repair as soon as you can. Wrapping the end with tape will also serve temporarily, and sealing with heat such as from a cigarette lighter may work though be careful of the melted end which can drip and burn. Whipping the end with twine will seal it if you have any twine to hand, and back splicing will also suffice if you know how to do it, though as this makes the end a little thicker it can become caught in cleats or on rings.

As a final point, lines that are frequently immersed in salt water can become stiff due to the build-up of salt. This makes them difficult to use, and a wash in fresh water will help to restore them.

FENDERS

Fenders are provided to help protect your yacht and whatever it comes into close contact with, be it another yacht, fishing boat or quay. Small fishing harbours can be crowded in season, and fenders are essential to prevent damage. One thing guaranteed to upset boat owners is seeing a yacht planning to come in alongside them that has not got its fenders out, so make sure they are in position well before you start to go into a vacant space.

Fender positions

When planning to tie up next to another boat or quay, position your fenders carefully. It is the widest part of the boat that normally takes most of the pressure (usually around the middle), but fenders will need to be spaced throughout its length as wind, sea swell and the wake of passing boats will cause it to move about and shift the points of contact. Check also how high your fenders need to be. If you plan to moor alongside a small fishing boat, for example, a fender tied too high will be of no use to either of you. Sometimes you will need to tie a fender lengthways to protect against posts protruding from a quay. Placing a fender under too much pressure can cause it to move out of position or even to pop out, leaving no protection at all.

Fenders do not always need to be tied on to serve a useful purpose. If mooring is difficult have a spare crew member dangle a mobile fender over the side on its lanyard. This is much safer and less painful than using a hand or foot to cushion any impact.

Securing fenders

Fenders can be tied on to the safety rails or stanchions. As charter companies usually charge for lost items, it is worth making sure they are tied on securely. When not in use, stow them so that they can be got out easily, perhaps in a cockpit locker. They get in the way if left dangling over the side or merely pulled up on deck while sailing, and are more likely to be lost overboard, besides which they never add much to your sea cred!

13 Boat Handling Under Power

BASIC ENGINE CHECKS

Inboard marine diesels are the engines of choice in the majority of charter yachts and there are a few basic checks you should carry out on the engine to help ensure trouble-free motoring. Take a good look at the engine when you first arrive so that you will be more likely to spot obvious faults if they occur later on. It is always a good policy to take a look at the engine before setting off each day, so as not to miss problems such as oil leaks.

All engines require a system of cooling. Although there are exceptions, the majority of marine diesel engines are water cooled. Many just use sea water, and some use fresh water that is in turn cooled by sea water in a heat exchanger. If the latter system is used, the level in the fresh water reservoir will need checking periodically. In both systems, sea water is drawn into the boat with a pump, via a fitting in the hull and through a water filter. Waste water leaves via the exhaust outlet: check whenever the engine is used that there is water coming out of it. It is also a good idea to check the water filter to make sure it is not becoming blocked with weed or other debris.

The engine oil level is checked with a dipstick. This is much easier on some engines than others, so always make sure to replace the dipstick correctly. Sometimes you will be unable to see where it came from, so keep a finger on the hole and replace it by feel. Check the level daily at least in the first couple of days to give an idea if or how much oil is being used, and if it is likely to need topping up at any point. To check the oil, remove the dipstick, wipe it clean, replace and remove it again and read off the level. Make sure that it stays between the two marks for high and low. Never try and check it with the engine running. Find out where to top up the oil should you need to.

The engine will have a water pump belt and an alternator belt, sometimes combined as one. Check they have not fallen off or become very slack.

The seal at the point where the propeller shaft goes through the hull is known as the stern gland.

The stern gland is where the propeller shaft exits through the hull. Find out if it needs greasing.

Many require no maintenance at all, though some need greasing periodically depending on engine use. If this is the case you should be shown how at the initial briefing.

Starting the engine

Always make sure you know how to stop an engine before you start it, just in case you have a problem such as finding it is in gear and not being able to get it out.

1.   Check that the cooling water intake seacock is turned on.

2.   Check that the fuel supply is turned on and that there is sufficient fuel in the tank.

3.   Check that the stop cable (if there is one) is pushed in ie is not in the stop position.

4.   Turn the battery changeover switch to the position for the engine battery. This is commonly position one. If there is no changeover switch, turn on the engine battery isolator switch.

Most yachts are fitted with at least two batteries, one dedicated to the engine and one to everything else. Some yachts are fitted with a changeover switch which allows you to use or charge one or the other or both at the same time. It is important to remember to

Make sure the engine stop cable (left) is pushed in before attempting to start.

A battery changeover switch. Position 2 is commonly used to connect the domestic supply battery.

switch off the engine battery when the engine is not in use so as not to drain it with other power demands. To make life easier, some yachts are fitted with a diode splitter which prevents the engine battery being used for anything else. There is no changeover switch, and charging is automatic for both batteries when the engine is running. Each battery has a separate isolator switch to turn it off and on.

5. Place the morse control in the correct position. Set the morse control with the gears in neutral, and the throttle in the fast running position.

The gear and throttle control levers are commonly called the morse control. Sometimes they consist of two separate levers, but frequently the controls are combined in one, and to disengage the gears but still use the throttle there will either be a button to press or release, or the whole lever will pull out or push in.

6. Utilise any cold-start system. Some diesel engines have mechanisms to aid starting, which use either heat or an excess fuel device. Some need using every time you start the engine, and others only when the engine is cold. Some newer engines do not have them at all, so find out if you have one and how and

when to use it.

7. Start the engine. Some controls have a key to turn as you would in a car. Some have three positions: *On, Heat, Start.* Others have only *On* and *Start.* Some controls use a key to turn on and a button to start, and others have only a button.

There will normally be oil pressure, charging and temperature warning lights on the control panel. Some have warning buzzers as well. Just as in a car, these should come on when the engine is switched on, and go off when the engine starts so that you know what they look and sound like when a fault occurs. To avoid panic if the lights or buzzer come on for any reason, make sure you know which is which from the start.

8. Adjust the throttle. As the engine starts, turn the throttle down to a fast idling speed while the engine warms up. If it is not given time to do so, it may stop when you put it into gear for the first time. This is usually at a vital moment having just pulled away from the quay, so check that the engine is running smoothly with the throttle turned down to the normal idling position before moving off.

A typical combined gear and throttle control in the upright neutral position. You push in the central button to take it out of gear.

An engine control panel with key. If sited in the cockpit, the panel should be well protected from the weather

9. Check that cooling water is coming from the exhaust. Sometimes excess fuel used to start the engine will cause smoke to appear from the exhaust as well. This should reduce as the engine warms up.

Running the engine

Before engaging a gear, make sure the engine is running at low revs. The sequence should be: low revs, into gear, increase revs. If the gears and throttle are combined in one lever you will have no choice, but it is still important to keep changes slow. Be kind to your gearbox and avoid going from full forwards to full reverse without giving the engine time to slow down to idling speed in neutral. In any case this will merely cause the water to cavitate around the propeller, you will lose drive and get a horrible bang from the gearbox.

The auxiliary engine on a yacht is not designed to be run at full throttle all of the time. You may even notice smoking from the exhaust with use of full throttle. A reduction in the revs will make very little difference to your boatspeed, and make considerable savings on fuel as well as being more environmentally friendly. It is also not good to leave the engine running at low revs and not working for any length of time.

To charge the batteries the engine needs to be running at least at a fast idle. If you have a changeover switch, this will regulate which battery is being charged. Leave it on *position one* for a while before switching to the *both* position in order to charge your domestic battery as well. If you have isolator switches, make sure they are both switched on. The diode splitter will automatically organise charging. Never turn the engine battery off while the engine is running, or damage to the alternator could result.

Turning the engine off

1. Reduce throttle to low revs and change gear into neutral. Let the engine idle for a few minutes before turning off.

2. Some engines have a stop cable that must be pulled, and some turn off at the key. If there is a stop cable, pull it until the engine has completely stopped, and then turn off the key. Make sure to push the stop cable back in again afterwards.

3. Turn off the engine battery switch, or switch over to the domestic battery.

Topping up the fuel tank

To check the level in the tank there may be either an

Start the engine with the button pushed in and the lever forwards. Returning the lever to the upright position releases the button and puts the engine into gear. Lever forward is forward gear, lever back is reverse gear, lever upright is neutral.

electrical gauge, a sight gauge or a dipstick. A sight gauge consists of a clear pipe sited near the tank in which the fuel level can be seen. The tank may be large enough for you not to have to top it up at all, but that depends on how much the engine is used. Monitoring the level each day will give you an idea how much you are using.

Some harbours and marinas have fuel quays. Your tanks are filled with a hose, just like filling a car. Diesel stains the decks, so have someone watch the gauge to call out how full it is getting to give you an idea when to slow down and stop. Frothing as it reaches the top can cause it to overflow, so slow down. Some tanks have an overflow pipe, so do not over-fill in case it spills out into the sea. Paper towels and washing up liquid should be ready in case of accidents.

You may need to top up with diesel from a container. Use a funnel with a filter if provided, and not the one for the water tanks. Avoid filling the funnel too full. It is always a good idea to have a spare container of fuel in the locker, and perhaps know the local word for 'diesel'.

Funnels used for topping up the fuel often have a built-in filter. Be careful not to muddle water and fuel funnels.

BOAT HANDLING

Drive is created by the engine turning the gearbox, and the gearbox turning the propeller shaft and propeller. The shaft turns one way in forwards and the other in reverse. Direction is controlled by the position of the rudder and the flow of water against it.

Learning how a yacht handles under power is basically a matter of practice. Some take a long time to slow down, some will turn very easily, and some need plenty of room. Yachts are never as responsive in reverse as in forwards and never as easy to handle. Do not be surprised if it takes a few days to feel confident because all yachts handle differently.

Prop-walk

Prop-walk describes the tendency of the propeller to move sideways through the water as it spins. Imagine each blade with a foot attached, walking in the direction of the turning propeller. Some boats are affected more than others, and the effect tends to be more pronounced in reverse. Practice to see which way the prop-walk takes you (if at all) in forwards and reverse. This needs to be compensated for when manoeuvring at close quarters, and when mastered can be even used to your advantage.

When manoeuvring astern, prop-walk can only be corrected if the boat is actually moving astern, otherwise it will merely swing in one direction or the other. As the boat starts to move, steer in the direction opposite to that of the walk, until the desired course is reached. Common mistakes are not allowing the yacht time to respond, and pushing the rudder over too far which reduces the steering effect. If possible give yourself plenty of room to manoeuvre.

Prop walk can be used to your advantage in a number of ways. It is often possible to turn the boat within its own length using short bursts of throttle in forwards and reverse. Start by moving forwards and turning in the direction the walk takes you when in reverse. Switch back to low revs and neutral, and allow the engine time to slow down before giving a burst astern. Continue with a burst forwards and back again until you have turned as required. Of course it is only possible to turn one way.

When coming alongside into a confined space, use the engine in reverse to walk the stern into the quay at the last minute. In a strong onshore wind, come in the other way and use the walk to keep you away from the quay. The same principle can help when leaving as well.

If you plan to moor stern-to and there is little room to correct the prop walk, it may be possible to start with the boat at an angle to the quay and use the walk to straighten you up. Do not be surprised if it takes a little time to learn these manoeuvres. Master the easier ones first.

TROUBLESHOOTING
Blocked water pump

Avoid taking things to bits unless you really have to. It may be a simple job to take the front off the water pump and have a look for a blockage, and you could try taking the intake pipe off the pump and blowing down it to see if it is clear. As a temporary emergency measure you could even try rigging up an alternative pump into the system such as the electric fresh water pump or a bilge pump.

Fault in the charging circuit

Low engine revs can cause the charging warning light to come on. Try increasing the revs a little and it should turn off. If not, switch off the engine and check

Prop-walking can be used to move a yacht in a confined space. If prop-walk throws the stern to the left, a short burst astern would move the yacht into its berth.

When reversing the helmsman should stand and face backwards so he can see where he is going. Keep movements of the rudder to a minimum, and do not attempt tight turns in reverse.

Left: Always check the exhaust outlet for cooling water, whenever the engine is running. Centre: The engine compartment is frequently under the companionway steps. Check to make sure the alternator belt is in place and not slack. Right: Water pump pulley and belt. Make sure the belt is in place.

for faults. Continuing to run the engine can damage the alternator.

Possible causes:
i)   Slipping alternator belt usually accompanied by a squealing noise – adjust if possible.
ii)   Alternator belt has fallen off – replace.
iii) Faulty connection in circuit such as the wires on the back of the alternator or a connection on the battery or diode splitter. Replace any that have obviously come adrift.

Engine will not start

1.   Check that you have followed the start procedure correctly and not omitted to turn anything on or to the correct position.
2.   Check that the stop cable is not in the stop position.
3.   Are you out of fuel?
4.   Is the battery flat? There may be a battery condition meter to tell you if the batteries are charged, charging, or both. You should also be able to hear if the battery is having trouble turning the engine over.

If you have a changeover switch, try using the domestic battery instead, and if that does not work try both together. If you have a diode splitter system, you can try swapping the batteries in case the engine battery is faulty. Some older engines have a starting handle. If so, make sure you are shown how to use it properly.

A flat engine battery can be caused by forgetting to switch it off, or by not switching over to the domestic supply. Excessive power usage will flatten a battery, such as leaving the fridge on for too long, or you may simply not have been using the engine long enough to charge the battery sufficiently. If there appears to be no problem with charging, a friendly neighbour may be able to connect you to their battery with a set of jump leads, or even lend you a battery for long enough to get the engine started. Make sure any connections go to the correct sides of the battery (red to red, black to black), and be careful of battery acid if you have to carry one from boat to boat. You will need to run the engine for about an hour to make sure the batteries are charged.

If the problem recurs or cannot be resolved, the circuit will need to be checked for faults.

5.   A problem with the cold-start system can also be a reason for non-starting, but will be a little harder to identify.

Engine stops

Possible causes:
i)   Fuel turned off?
ii)   Out of fuel or low on fuel? If the fuel is low and the boat heels, air can be sucked into the system with the same result.
iii) Fouled propeller (a rope or fishing net)?
iv) Serious lack of oil and overheating will also cause an engine to stop!

Bleeding the engine

If you are low on fuel or run out air will enter the system and the engine will stop or refuse to start. Unlike a petrol engine the problem will not be resolved simply by filling the tank, unless you are lucky enough to have an engine with a self-bleeding system. If you catch the problem just in time and stop the engine before it dies completely, you may get away with filling the tank and restarting. If not you will have to bleed the system.

Bleeding the engine means removing any air in the line, from fuel tank at one end to injectors at the other. The first step is being able to identify the parts of the engine relevant to the job in hand. When on bareboat charter, if you are practically minded and think you can cope with it, you can ask for instruction as to how to bleed this particular engine. You may also be provided with a manual. By far the best policy of course is NEVER TO LET THE TANK BECOME LOW OR RUN OUT OF FUEL IN THE FIRST PLACE.

It is not possible here to say exactly what you will find, but most diesels operate on the same basic principles. Throughout the fuel line there will be pumps and filters, but not always in the same order or of the same type and number. It may be possible to follow the line as it travels from the tank to the engine, and deal with whatever you find on the way.

First put fuel in the tank and make sure that it is turned on. Air will need to be released progressively through the system, starting at the end nearest the tank. Filters and some pumps will have a screw or nut on the top with a washer underneath. This is known as a bleed nipple and must be loosened to release any air.

If the fuel leaves the tank due to gravity, the first thing that it may come to is a coarse filter or water separator or both combined as one. To free any air from this filter, loosen the bleed nipple on top and allow any air to escape. Retighten the nipple when fuel comes through instead. Be careful not to over-tighten, as this could strip the threads.

Next along the line will be the fuel lift pump. Sometimes this is used to suck fuel from the tank rather than just relying on gravity. If this is the case, any filter between it and the tank will not need bleeding. Sometimes this pump can be operated by hand with a lever on the side, but other times it must be operated by turning the engine electrically with the key. To avoid flattening the battery by continued turning, the decompression lever (or levers) situated on top of the cylinder/s should be operated before turning the engine. Sometimes there will be a decompression lever for each cylinder, but usually only one for them all. The fuel lift pump does not require bleeding.

After the fuel lift pump will come one or more filters. Each one must be bled in turn. Loosen the bleed nipple on the first filter and use the fuel lift pump to release any air. Retighten the nipple and move on to the next.

After the filters will come the injection pump/s which pump fuel to the injector/s. Each cylinder has its own injector and injection pump. First bleed the injection pump/s using the fuel lift pump as before. All the injection pumps can be bled at the same time.

Finally air must be released from the pipe leading from the injection pump/s to the injector/s. Loosen the connection where the pipe meets the injector, and use the injection pump to release the air. The injection pump must be operated by turning the engine in the full throttle position. All these pipes can be bled at the same time. A twelve cylinder twin engine motor boat could take some time! Return the decompression lever to its original position and try to start the engine. Sometimes the bleeding process will have to be repeated before the engine will start.

Water in the fuel

The first thing that water does if placed in the fuel tank is sink to the bottom. This means that it will be the first thing to enter the fuel line when the engine is next started up. If it gets to the injectors, they will rust and seize. Injectors and injection pumps are precision pieces of equipment and will not tolerate misuse. If you realise your mistake, DO NOT start the engine, and seek professional help. The tank will need to be drained completely, and refilled with fresh diesel when it is certain all the water has been removed. If the engine has been started, filters in the fuel line will need to be changed and the system flushed through with fresh fuel.

As an emergency measure, if the engine has not been started, it may be possible to utilise an alternative fuel supply by turning off the fuel tap at the tank, taking off the pipe at the start of the fuel line where it meets the tap, and putting it into a spare canister of diesel instead, being careful not to get any air into it at the same time. This could allow you to use the engine for a limited time to get out of a difficult situation.

Fuel in the water

Most water system piping is plastic, as are many water tanks. We know of no successful method of removing the smell and taste of diesel from water systems after contamination, and getting rid of the diesel from the tanks to start with is no easy matter. Stainless steel tanks can be taken out and steam cleaned, but plastic tanks and piping will need replacing.

Water pump seals will be destroyed by diesel, so be careful when filling the tank, or you could be buying a lot of bottled water.

OTHER PROBLEMS
VHF radio will not work

Low battery power? The radio will only operate on high power if there is sufficient power in the battery. Turn on the engine and give enough revs to activate charging – this will cure the problem almost immediately if the battery was the cause.

Fridge will not work

Electric fridges normally exert quite a drain on battery power, and usually require a reasonably well-charged battery to kick them into life when first turned on. If the fridge fails to respond when switched on, try turning on the engine to give the batteries a boost.

14 Mooring

In British harbours and marinas, mooring is often alongside a quay, pontoon or another yacht. Many estuaries are scattered with laid moorings, with boats tied between them or swinging with the tide, perhaps sitting on the mud at low water. In the Mediterranean, where mooring is unaffected by any tide to speak of, bows-to or stern-to mooring is the norm in harbours and marinas alike. Idyllic bays around Greece, Turkey and the Virgin Islands (which also have minimal tides) are perfect sites for dropping the bow anchor, and either sitting bows to the wind or taking a stern line ashore, knowing that you will not be left high and dry on the sand in the morning.

TYPES OF MOORING
Bows-to or stern-to a quay

This is common in harbours where quay space is limited.

General Advantages
1.   There is no need for anyone to be tramping over your yacht at all hours to get to their own boat.
2.   You are less likely to receive unwanted guests such as cockroaches. If this is a problem, avoid bringing cardboard boxes on board with the shopping. If moored stern-to, take up the boarding ladder *(passerelle)* at night to help deter rodents. Thread the top half of a plastic bottle onto the mooring line to act as a further deterrent.

Advantages of bows-to mooring
1.   Allows privacy as no one can peer into the companionway from the quay.
2.   Bows-to mooring is your only option when the sea bed shallows up to the quay with rocks and all sorts of hazards just under the water. You would damage your rudder and keel if you were to try and moor stern-to or alongside.
3.   It is the easiest of the two methods to learn, as yachts are not as easy to steer when driving astern and can steer to one side.

Moored bows-to, hold onto something firm such as the forestay and pulpit when climbing on board.

Advantages of stern-to mooring
1.   Larger yachts are usually fitted with a stern passerelle which makes getting on and off easier.
2.   Larger yachts are also usually fitted with a winch for the bow anchor, as the ground tackle must be heavy enough to give adequate holding power. A similar-sized tackle on the stern would be difficult to handle so the line is frequently of rope rather than chain, often making the bow anchor the choice where holding is concerned.

Where will you moor?

A local pilot guide will give advice about the type of mooring you will find and where it will be safe to moor. It is always advisable to keep a lookout on the bow to let you know if you come too near other anchor lines or mooring buoys, or are about to go aground as it is often easy to see the bottom.

The stern ladder or 'passerelle' is a useful feature on a larger yacht, but can obviously only be used stern-to from the transom to the quay.

There's no hurry. Always take it slowly when approaching an unfamiliar quay, and if you are not sure stand off until you have made up your mind.

Take it slow when approaching an unfamiliar mooring, as the presence of a quay is by no means an indication that it is possible to moor there. It may be intended for small boats, or even none at all. Avoid places obviously used by local boats with piles of fishing nets on the quay, or the local ferry berth. Be careful of local laid moorings which may be buoyed by a plastic bottle accompanied by floating lines.

These moorings are not normally intended for use by visiting yachts, besides which you do not know the state of the ground tackle.

If there is plenty of choice don't take up three spaces when one will do and try and leave deep quay space for deep draught boats. Harbours are not necessarily safe from all directions of wind and waves, so try and choose your spot carefully. Marinas may

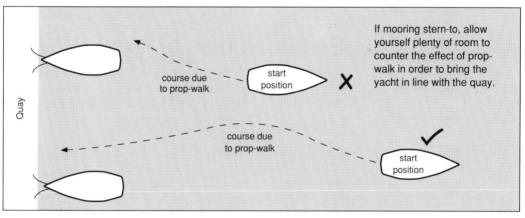

If mooring stern-to, allow yourself plenty of room to counter the effect of prop-walk in order to bring the yacht in line with the quay.

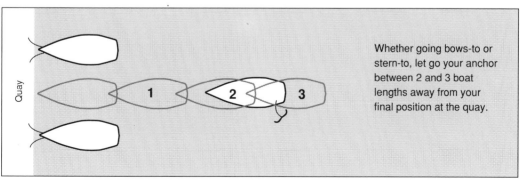

Whether going bows-to or stern-to, let go your anchor between 2 and 3 boat lengths away from your final position at the quay.

have visitors' berths, but if not, pick a space and find out afterwards where you should go. It is common to find fixed mooring lines in marinas and some more developed harbours throughout the Mediterranean and you are usually expected to use them. Beware of using your own anchor as it will probably become fouled on the many lines of chain on the sea bed, and be impossible to retrieve without a diver.

The approach

Having decided where you would like to go, make sure that your crew know what you intend to do, what needs to be done, and by whom. Be prepared in advance by having your sails down and stowed, and fenders and lines positioned and ready. Although in theory it should be possible to sail into a space, in practice you will be very unpopular with other boat owners, who would expect you to have your engine running at the very least.

Look out for anchor lines, and keep well clear. This is no time to foul your propeller. Avoid excessive speed when approaching the quay. You will need to have a good idea how the boat will handle under power and whether you need plenty of space for it to slow down. If there is a strong headwind you may

need more speed. If there is a nasty side-wind you may need to position the boat upwind to allow for drift. These effects are increased if the boat is very light or presents a lot of surface to the wind. If you are mooring stern-to, give yourself plenty of room to counter the effect of prop-walk.

Letting go

Aim to let go your anchor two to three boat lengths away from your final position at the quay, depending on the depth of water. If there is any chain, be careful not to let it rattle out: considerable damage can be done by chain on gelcoat. On the bow, run the chain over the roller; on the stern run the chain over the metal rubbing plate, if there is one. If not, coil the chain in a bucket and feed it out from there.

If the length of chain is short, you may need to pay it out by hand first before letting go as you come to rope. Coming in slowly allows you time to leave the helm for a second to throw the anchor out if you are short of crew. It is important to make sure the line is going to run free, or the anchor may crash into the boat on its way down. Alternatively you may prefer to have the anchor trailing out behind you ready to go. Be aware that some anchors will fly near the surface of the water, and with any speed will sea-saw from side to side which is a hazard to the wide stern of a modern yacht.

If the sea bed drops quite steeply away from the shore and you drop the stern anchor too soon, you may run out of line before you reach the quay. If you do run out of line, and there is no danger of drifting onto other boats or anchor lines, leave the engine in neutral, pull a length of line back on board and tie a bowline in it. A further length of line can then be attached with another bowline or a double sheet bend,

Probably the best method of releasing the stern anchor is to throw it over the stern, ensuring the line will run free.

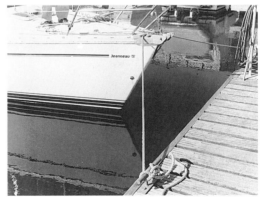

Leave enough slack on the bow lines to keep the yacht well off the quay in all conditions

To form a slip line for getting away, keep one end attached to a cleat on deck, take the other end through a ring or round a bollard on the quay, and bring the line back on board.

Look out for the anchor on its way up when leaving a bows-to mooring. Take care to keep it clear of the sides of the yacht as you lift it up onto the stern and stow the chain and line.

and paid out as you motor forwards into your space. Be careful to keep all slack line inboard if you drift backwards while joining the lines.

Do not rely totally on either your anchor line or reverse gear to stop you as you reach the quay. The anchor may not take hold and the engine has been known to fail at crucial moments. Remember that many propellers are inefficient with the engine in reverse.

Is the anchor holding?

Having secured all your lines, do not just dump everything in relief and reach for the gin and tonics. Make sure your anchor is holding well. If it cannot be made tight from the stern (it just keeps coming when you pull) you will need to relay it with the dinghy. A bow anchor which has a lot of heavy chain is almost impossible to row out, so you will need to have another go at mooring.

To relay the anchor from the stern with a dinghy, ask your neighbour if you can attach a spring line from your boat to his to hold you off the quay temporarily.

Pull the anchor back on board, after which it can be lowered into the dinghy with any rope or chain and rowed out again, with the line being paid out from the boat as you go. Drop any chain and finally the anchor, being careful not to damage the dinghy with the pointed flukes and making sure you don't become entangled in it all on the way down. When it has had time to settle on the sea bed, take up the tension again from the stern.

Sometimes anchor holding can be poor due to silting so allow it half an hour or so to sink-in before tensioning completely, making sure you do not hit the quay in the meantime. Laying a second anchor may be a wise precaution if you cannot get a very good hold.

To make sure your anchor will hold you off the quay in the event of any onshore wind, swell or wake from passing boats (which can be considerable), stand on the quay, take hold of the boat and pull as hard as you can. If the bow or stern will touch the quay, you are too near, so loosen the mooring lines, tension up the anchor and try again. More room must

Mooring side-on to a quay means you can just step off the side of the yacht. You should not need to leap for the quay before you get there.

be given when moored stern-to as your rudder is vulnerable near the quay. There may be sufficient depth when the sea is calm, but not with the surge from a passing ship.

Leaving the mooring

When leaving a bows-to or stern-to mooring, avoid putting the engine into gear until you are well clear of all anchor lines and ideally until your own is back on board; or if you were using a fixed mooring line, until it has had time to sink after being thrown clear. Only use the engine to stop yourself being blown off course if you are sure the propeller is clear.

Mooring side-on

You may have to moor alongside if anchor holding is poor, if the marina uses finger pontoons or if all that is left is to come alongside another boat. If there is anyone on board, ask if it is OK to do so. If there is no one there, tie up and ask when they come back and also ask when they next plan to leave. As long as their boat is not a lot smaller and you make sure your fenders are well positioned, they probably won't mind. Take additional lines ashore so as not to rely entirely on their mooring lines. You may want to put all your fenders onto one side as you come in, repositioning some once you're secure.

If you are short on crew and there is a strong offshore wind blowing, try to get one line secured from your bow to the shore at a point near your stern. Then use the engine to drive the boat forward and steer towards the quay. This will hold the boat close

Coming alongside another yacht. Always make sure they are happy to receive you, and are a suitable size. In particular the yacht on the inside should not be much shorter. Ask permission whenever you wish to cross over.

A well protected anchorage with the yachts held fast by stern lines to the shore to prevent them blowing around.

Some advocate flaking the anchor chain and warp on the foredeck prior to dropping it to prevent any tangles.

until the other lines can be tied. A similar technique can be used when leaving the quay. The stern can be made to swing out by driving forward on a spring from the bow, and the bow made to move out by driving backwards on a spring from the stern. Use slip lines as springs as these will be easier to release as you leave.

ANCHORING

Some harbours allow for anchoring off, though others may be too small for this to be practical. Anchoring in a bay is very popular in Greece, and even more so in Turkey where harbours are fewer. Anchoring-off is extremely common throughout the Caribbean and in many other parts of the world.

Frequently a stern line or anchor is taken ashore, which allows more boats to moor because no one needs room to swing. Holding may be improved by keeping the bow pointed towards the entrance of a bay if you expect unpleasant wind or swells to appear. Holding is disadvantaged if the wind blows onto the beam however as the boat cannot swing into it, and neither will it be very comfortable on board. Mark your stern line with a fender so it can be seen by other boats.

Choosing an anchorage

When choosing an anchorage check to see how other yachts are moored. Look out for stern lines that are preventing them from swinging. Are you exposed to any wind direction? If so, pick a sheltered spot. Try to estimate how far and in what direction you might swing, and allow yourself plenty of room from the shore and other boats. If possible try and pick a suitable spot on the sea bed such as a sandy patch as opposed to weed or rock, and if there is coral avoid it with both anchor and line. Chain may be safe from damage by coral, but warp is not.

You need to be sure you have sufficient scope of line to anchor in any particular place. As a rough guide lay at least three or four times the depth of chain, and five or six times the depth of warp. The more you lay out, the better the holding will be, because any pulling or jerking will be dampened before it reaches the anchor. The weight of the line, especially chain, complements that of the anchor. Even if your anchor line is of warp, there will probably be a short length of chain nearest the anchor which helps to keep it in a horizontal position on the sea bed, and helps it to stay dug in. A deep anchorage for which you have too short a line may be OK for a short stay such as lunch stop, as long as you are prepared to keep a good eye on your position.

Laying the anchor

To lay the anchor, approach head-to-wind, and allow

Rafting up can be so very nice to do, but is only successful in a well protected anchorage in calm weather. At the merest hint of trouble, the yachts should move apart and anchor separately with room to swing.

the boat to come to a stop before dropping the anchor. Even better, if you have just started to move astern the line will lay out on the sea bed rather than dropping into a heap beneath you. It may be possible to let the wind take you backwards, though you may need to use the engine as well. Do not be surprised if you find the boat being swung round side-on to the wind as the line is laid out. It will come back round into the wind again after a while.

To test the anchor, motor astern and see if it stops you. This should also help it to take hold. If it appears to be dragging, try laying out some more line and testing it again. Take compass bearings of points on the shore to give you an idea of your position so you know if you move. If you are concerned about holding, as long as there are not going to be any major changes in tidal direction, it may be advisable to lay a second anchor at 45 degrees to the first using the dinghy, though you may have a bit of untangling to do

when it comes to bringing the lines in if there have been any windshifts during the night.

You may be able to check the anchor by taking a swim and having a look if visibility is good. If the sea bed is rocky, you may want to rig a trip line to the crown of the anchor in case the flukes become fouled on the bottom. Either take the end back to the boat, or tie a fender to it and let it float above the anchor. If you are likely to swing much in the night, the latter is best since it will not become tangled with the anchor line, but it is more of a hazard to other yachts.

ALTERNATIVE MOORINGS
Buoys

Some harbours and anchorages offer laid moorings to visiting yachts as an alternative to swinging on anchor. The buoys will usually be labelled as such, or a pilot guide may give advice on which ones to use.

Piles

You may encounter piles to tie between. Attach yourself to one with a slip rope and then drive backwards or forwards to the other, after which you can position yourself between the two. Be careful to take into account any effect wind or tide may have before negotiating this kind of mooring.

Sometimes a pile is used to hold you off the quay. Attach a slip line as you go past and bring it back on board. This will make it easier when the time comes to leave.

Double-ups

When quay space is scarce yachts on flotilla may be asked to moor bows-to the stern of another yacht or yachts. The principle is the same as mooring bows-to a quay, but greater care needs to be taken of other anchor lines which will run almost beneath you. Make sure to steer between them, and then secure your bow to the other stern (or sterns). This may require some agility on the part of your crew unless there is someone on board to pass the lines to. Again it is a good idea to take a line ashore as well. This type of mooring allows less privacy to the yacht in front. If climbing on and off the bow is not your strong point, it may be easier to row ashore in the dinghy.

Rafting

On flotilla you may need to raft up – at a barbecue, for example. To save space several yachts are moored in line, with bow anchors into the bay and stern lines or anchors to shore. Breast and spring lines between the boats help to prevent excessive movement and to spread uneven loads. Stagger the masts to prevent the spreaders and rigging clashing in the swell or wash from passing traffic.

PART THREE

KEEPING OUT OF TROUBLE

15 Safety

The skipper must be responsible for all aspects of safety where yacht and crew are concerned. Charter yachts should comply with certain basic regulations depending on where they are chartered, and companies should make it their business to ensure that standards are maintained. It is advisable to check out safety equipment when you arrive, so as to be sure of what there is, and that it is in good working order. There often is no time for staff to check every single detail between charters, and if the previous crew have done something strange to the equipment on board, such as allowed the flares to get wet or used the batteries from the man overboard lights or torch to run their ghetto blaster, it may be up to you to find out what the problems are.

Simple checks

• Check that the liferings and lines are not tangled up. If you have a liferaft, check that it is tied on at the painter. Liferafts usually inflate due to the action of pulling on the painter as the container is thrown into the water. The painter also prevents it from floating away. If you have no liferaft, it is because the sailing area is not considered to demand it, and an inflated dinghy is carried instead.

The situation must be very serious indeed before you consider abandoning the yacht: even a severely disabled boat can provide more security than a liferaft. In the case of a serious fire, launching the liferaft in readiness may be a good idea to prevent it being damaged should you need it.

Whatever the yacht, the skipper is responsible for the safety of those on board. A charter is not always in the warm waters of the Mediterranean, and a colder coastline can be an altogether less forgiving environment.

Safety harnesses should be where you know you can find them. Get used to putting them on, and if in doubt always wear them.

A lifering can help keep a person afloat, and also make it easier to find them. Some have a buoy with a flag attached.

There may also be a drogue to stop the lifering drifting, and a flashing light which self-activates to help with identification at night.

• Powder fire extinguishers can be checked by shaking to make sure the powder is not solid, and checking the pressure gauge if there is one. Flares, life jackets and harnesses should be easily to hand if needed, but avoid stowing them where they can get wet.

• Major leaks on a boat are rare. But think ahead and check the whereabouts and operation of all bilge pumps (both electric and manual) as well as the places where leaks are most likely to occur, such as at piping to seacocks, the stern gland, and instrument transducers that exit through the hull.

• Always be careful of inspecting an engine when in operation. Keep yourself and your clothing away from all moving parts. Unless it is essential to observe the engine in action, turn it off before removing the inspection panel.

Preventing emergencies

An important aspect of safety is teaching the crew what to do in the event of an emergency, and indeed many worry about what to do if something were to happen to the skipper. Inexperienced crew will be unaware of hazards such as being hit by the boom in a gybe, or of getting their fingers trapped by lines on a cleat or winch.

Avoid problems by making sure that the deck is clear of lines, and that roller furling headsail sheets are cleated off so that they do not give way as you grab hold of them when getting back on board at the end of an evening. Try to recognise when your crew are feeling tired, ill or apprehensive. They are on holiday after all. It is a good idea to decide on a few ground rules such as when harnesses should be worn. A harness is a good idea if someone is being sick over the side, and probably does not care at that precise moment if they live or die. All this may seem a little unnecessary when you are enjoying a relaxing, calm sail between idyllic islands, but there may be times when you will be glad you gave it some thought.

Navigation

Careful navigation and passage planning are also an important part of safety. A skipper should never be drunk in charge, even when in harbour or at anchor. It is tempting to forget in the evenings when alcohol is plentiful, but you never know when it will be necessary to get up in the night because the wind has picked up or your anchor is dragging. It is then that you must have your wits about you.

16 Keeping Watch

Keep a proper look-out at all times. When visibility is good, scan the horizon every few minutes to check for other vessels in the area. Large ships move surprisingly fast and can creep up on you unawares. Fishing nets are often marked with small buoys or improvised ones made of polystyrene or plastic bottles. The nets themselves are usually well below the surface, but the buoyed ends can easily be lost to view in the trough of a wave. You also need to steer round floating debris such as fishing crates and oil drums. Passenger liners and local ferries often frequent the areas popular with yachts so watch for them on recognised routes.

The crew can help to keep watch especially if the helmsman's view is partially obstructed by the sails, or if visibility is poor. Do not assume a small yacht can always be seen by others. In the unlikely event of fog,

keep a listening watch, perhaps with someone on the bow where other engines will be heard more clearly. It may be necessary to switch the engine off every so often to listen and if in a shipping route move away as quickly as possible.

Safe speed

A safe speed is one that allows a vessel time to take action to avoid a collision.

Will we collide?

There is a risk of collision if, over a period of time, there is no appreciable change in the compass bearing of an approaching vessel. Check this by taking a series of bearings with a hand-bearing compass. Another easy way of checking is to first keep a steady course, then line the vessel up with something on your yacht such as a stanchion or shroud. If it stays in line, not moving much in relation to you, then there is no change in bearing and you are likely to collide.

Keep watch with a clear view forward at all times. Assess where other yachts are heading, and if in doubt take avoiding action.

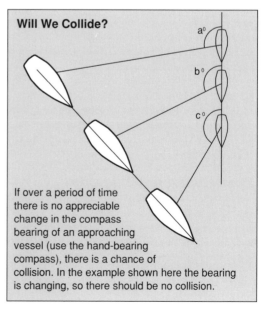

Will We Collide?

a⁰

b⁰

c⁰

If over a period of time there is no appreciable change in the compass bearing of an approaching vessel (use the hand-bearing compass), there is a chance of collision. In the example shown here the bearing is changing, so there should be no collision.

What are their intentions?

Any vessel approached by another will want to know what it intends to do, regardless of who has right of way. The rules state that any action taken should be positive and made in ample time. Small alterations of course will often only serve to confuse the situation. From a distance, a definite 90 degree turn to port or starboard will not be misunderstood. But do make the turn early.

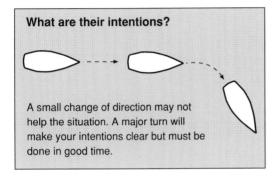

What are their intentions?

A small change of direction may not help the situation. A major turn will make your intentions clear but must be done in good time.

If you are the vessel with right of way, keep a steady course and speed to help the other to determine your intentions. But it is also your responsibility to ensure a collision does not occur, so do not just doggedly continue until it is too late to get out of the way. The other vessel may not have seen you, or might not know the rules.

Narrow channels

When negotiating a narrow channel, vessels must keep as near to the starboard side as is safe and practicable. In this way boats pass port-to-port, and the centre of the channel is normally left to larger vessels which may find manoeuvring difficult and which may have no option but to pass down the middle due to their draft.

All vessels under 20 metres (65 feet), even if sailing, must not impede them in any way.

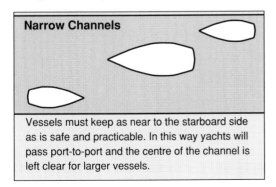

Narrow Channels

Vessels must keep as near to the starboard side as is safe and practicable. In this way yachts will pass port-to-port and the centre of the channel is left clear for larger vessels.

Sailing Vessels

When two boats under sail approach each other, the rules determine who has to give way.

Port and Starboard
When two yachts meet on opposite tacks, port tack always gives way. Port tack gives way (wind on port side; mainsail to starboard). Starboard tack has right of way (wind on starboard side; mainsail to port).

Port tack gives way

Same Tack
When yachts meet on the same tack, the windward boat must keep clear. Here both boats are on starboard, and A (nearer the wind) must keep clear.

1. Port tack gives way to starboard tack.
2. If both boats are on the same tack, a second rule applies - windward boat keeps clear.
3. It is not always possible to be sure which tack another boat is on. In this case the rule is to assume she is on starboard, and give way accordingly.

In the case of windsurfers, even if you have right of way it is often better to be on the safe side and give them a wide berth unless they are obviously well in control.

Power-driven vessels

Power-driven vessels that are restricted in manoeuvrability in some way (such as having a deep draft or being engaged in fishing) have right of way over sailing vessels as well as over other power-driven craft. Those not restricted are required to give way to those under sail. In practice large power-driven vessels cannot always be relied upon or even expected to give way to every sailing yacht. A ferry on its daily route from A to B has a job to do and life is made much easier if sailing yachts aim to keep clear.

NB. A sailing yacht that is using its engine, either alone

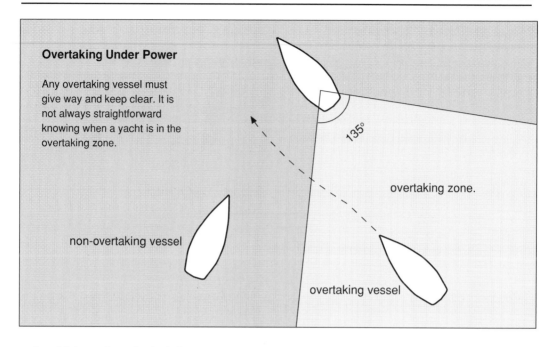

Overtaking Under Power

Any overtaking vessel must give way and keep clear. It is not always straightforward knowing when a yacht is in the overtaking zone.

135°

overtaking zone.

non-overtaking vessel

overtaking vessel

or in addition to its sails, is defined as a power-driven vessel.

Close encounters

The rules state what power-driven vessels must do in the event of overtaking, crossing and meeting one another head-on. The rules are straightforward enough, but difficulty sometimes comes when trying to decide in which category a situation falls:

1. *Overtaking – an overtaking boat keeps clear.*
    Any vessel overtaking another must give way, and

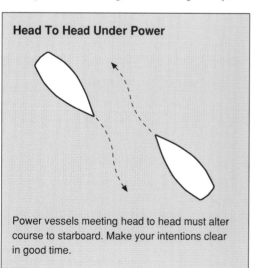

Head To Head Under Power

Power vessels meeting head to head must alter course to starboard. Make your intentions clear in good time.

keep clear until well away from the situation. Sailing vessels are not exempt even when overtaking a vessel under power. It is not always easy to decide exactly where the overtaking zone is, though at night the stern light of the overtaken vessel makes the situation clearer.

2. *Vessels meeting head to head.*
    Power vessels approaching each other head-on must change course to starboard, passing port side to port side. This is a situation where it's wise to make your intentions clear in good time. If in doubt as to whether this is a head to head or crossing situation, it is safer to assume the former and alter course to starboard. At night the situation is made simpler by lights. If you can see both port and starboard lights of an approaching vessel, it is facing you head-on. If it is a vessel over 50 metres (165 feet) long, its steaming lights will be in line as well.

3. *Crossing – a vessel gives way to another on its starboard side.*
    In the situation in the diagram, boat A must give way. (At night the red port side light of boat B will be visible.) The best action is for A to alter course to starboard and pass astern of B. Altering course to port and passing ahead of B would require plenty of time. If B, as the vessel with right of way, is unsure of the intentions of A she should always alter course to starboard to avoid a collision.

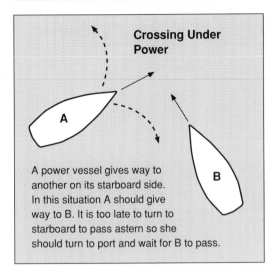

Crossing Under Power

A power vessel gives way to another on its starboard side. In this situation A should give way to B. It is too late to turn to starboard to pass astern so she should turn to port and wait for B to pass.

Sound signals

You may encounter a few sound signals. Ferries frequenting the same harbours as yachts may use them when manoeuvring in and out. One short blast (1 sec) indicates a change of course to starboard, two a change to port, and three tells you that their engines are running astern though they may not be moving astern as yet. If a yacht shows no sign of taking avoiding action, it will probably be met by five or more short blasts which is basically the signal to get out of the way, or at least to make your intentions clear, though scarpering is probably the wisest move.

Charter yachts usually carry a horn which may be hand or aerosol operated. In the event of restricted visibility, a yacht that is sailing must give one long blast (4-6 secs) followed by two short blasts every two minutes. A vessel travelling under power must give one long blast every two minutes.

Distress signals

Several signals may be used to indicate that a vessel or its crew is in distress and that assistance is required. Some of these are listed below:

1. The word MAYDAY on a radio telephone.
2. Continuous sounding of a foghorn.
3. Red flares – rocket, parachute or hand-held.
4. Orange smoke flares.
5. Slow repeated raising and lowering of the arms
6. Morse SOS (··· – – – ···) by any means.

NB. White hand flares are used to draw the attention of another vessel when there is a risk of collision.

17 Basic Navigation

You don't need anything big or fancy to navigate with, and the equipment on a small yacht should be more than sufficient. Time spent studying the chart and familiarising yourself with the day's sailing reaps dividends when it comes to finding the way, which is particularly important if you are short handed.

WHAT YOU NEED

Some cruising areas require only a basic knowledge and experience of navigational skills, whereas others demand an ability to get from A to B as and when you want to, despite varying tidal heights and streams and being away from the sight of land.

Navigation aids and equipment will be included in the inventory on board any yacht, though will vary as to their number and sophistication. For most holiday purposes the basics will be perfectly sufficient and those listed below are what you would hope to have at the very least. Read the company literature to find out if there is anything else you want or need to take with you.

Items normally included:
VHF radio.
Chart(s).

Pilot Guide (perhaps only basic).
Plotter – parallel rules, Breton plotter, etc.
Dividers.
Hand-bearing compass.
Cockpit compass.
Pencils, rubber, sharpener.
Tidal information – if applicable.

Items frequently provided:
Log.
Echo sounder.
Wind speed and direction instruments.
Decca and Loran in areas where signals are received.

Items becoming more common:
Global Positioning System (GPS).
Navtex (weather, navigational and safety information).

Are you sure there's enough water under the keel? Don't go steaming along unless you are absolutely certain.

Items on top yachts:

Others items such as forward-looking sonar, Single Side Band radio (SSB), weather fax, radar and even on-board computers are likely only to be found on larger skippered yachts, being limited by cost, power supply, operator skill and licence requirements.

CHARTS

Much inshore navigation is about being able to see where you are going. A chart allows you to make sense of what you are seeing and work out where you are, as well as telling you what lies beneath the water. You will need to know how to interpret this information to avoid anything solid and dangerous such as a rocky shoal. (We did hear of a couple who managed to find their way by boat round Sardinia using only a Michelin road map. Either they were very careful or very lucky!)

Much of the data will be irrelevant to small vessels such as yachts. For instance, a wreck out to sea 10 metres below the surface in non-tidal waters is not going to do you any harm, unless you plan to take up trawling. Recognising just what is important is the first step.

The British Admiralty Hydrographic Department produces charts for most parts of the world, and they are principally designed for use by naval and commercial vessels, but others such as yachtsmen are able to benefit as well. Symbols and abbreviations are used to describe physical features, and the Admiralty publication 5011 explains what they all mean.

Local charts

You may be provided with a British Admiralty chart when visiting countries such as Greece, but many nations produce their own. In the Caribbean the charts provided may be those of the US National Ocean Survey or US Defence Mapping Agency. The French Navicarte produced by Cartographiques Maritimes is available for all French coastlines and some nearby such as North Sardinia and the Balearics, as well as booklet versions for all inland waterways.

THE DEPTH

Check whether the depths are in metres or fathoms. Not all charts have been updated to the metric system as yet. Fathom charts are in black and white. The depth of water in any particular place, most notably in tidal waters, is constantly changing. Even in the Mediterranean, water levels are not completely constant as very slight tides and changes in atmospheric pressure still have some effect. What you can be almost totally sure of is that they will never fall below that given on a chart (known as chart datum).

In the Mediterranean, changes in depth are insignificant enough to do away with the need for tidal data, and to estimate the depth of water in any particular place you need do no more than look at the chart. In tidal areas, tidal data allows you to work out how much higher than chart datum the water level will be at any particular time, on any particular day of the year.

It pays to have a good idea as to how deep your

yacht is below the waterline (how much it draws). In practice, do not take chances by trying to go where there is only just enough depth. You may have miscalculated your position, or find yourself taken off course by an on-shore breeze. Not every minor variation in depth will be marked, and depths will be less in the trough of a wave. If you can see the sea bed beneath you, practice estimating how deep it is and checking with the echo sounder (depth meter). Depths in water can be very misleading.

Echo sounders

Echo sounders operate by measuring how long it takes a signal to travel from a transducer in the hull to the sea bed below and back again. It helps to have an idea where the transducer is situated, and how much of the boat lies beneath it. Some have little idiosyncrasies like switching to 0.7 metres when in very deep water, or to zero at the vital moment when you think you might be in danger of going aground.

Think about where you are. There may be no shallow areas for miles. It may help to take a look over the side. Check that there is no alternative scale you should have switched to, but do not ignore the echo sounder if there is any possibility it could be right. There may be an alarm setting to warn you when water is getting shallow, so set it for at least a few metres beneath your keel as it only 'sees' what is beneath you and not what is ahead.

If all else fails and you do not have a lead line on board, make your own by tying something heavy onto the end of a piece of line and dangling it over the side until it touches the bottom.

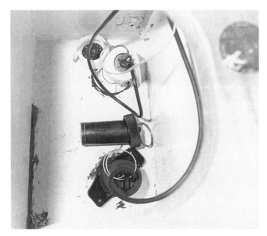

The log and echo sounder transducer exit through the hull. Note the plugs, which are used to fill the holes if necessary.

THE DISTANCE

To work out how long it will take you to reach a destination, first find out how far it is. Use the dividers to measure the distance on the chart. Transfer them over to the latitude scale immediately opposite (the latitude scale runs vertically along the sides of the chart, from north to south) and read off how many minutes lie between its points. (Do not use the longitude scale on the bottom and top of the chart.)

Degrees and minutes are the units used. Each degree is divided up into 60 minutes, and each minute of latitude at that level on the chart represents one nautical mile (slightly longer than a land mile). If the distance is too great for the dividers to reach, or you need to alter course somewhere on the way, set the dividers to a distance such as 5 miles, and walk them over the chart from one point to the next.

Speed

Next you need to know how fast you will go. This will be influenced by the direction and strength of the wind, the sails and how well you set them, whether you use the engine, whether there are any tidal streams to take into account, and whether you decide to stop for lunch on the way.

All yachts have an optimum speed through the water depending on their size and design. Water resistance will mean that they are rarely able to go above this speed, whatever they do (unless surfing down waves with a following wind). An average cruising speed for a 32 foot (10 metre) yacht is 5 to 6 knots. One knot = one nautical mile per hour. Speed x time = distance, so at a speed of 5 knots in three hours you will travel a distance of 15 nautical miles.

Use the log

It is unlikely that you will keep a constant speed throughout the entire journey so you can only estimate your journey time. During the trip you will want to estimate how far you have travelled so refer to the log and keep a regular record of your speed. Many logs will give both speed and distance travelled through the water (the trip mode on electronic logs).

Many logs work by means of a small paddle wheel on the under-side of the hull which turns as the water passes over it. Sometimes they become clogged with weed and no longer turn, giving you a zero reading on the display. Next time you go for a swim, dive underneath and clear it. This is a simpler operation than taking it out from inside the boat, as long as the water is not too cold! Try practising estimating your speed so that you can have a rough idea how far you

Plotting the course is easy at a flotilla briefing when the support team can tell you where to go and how long it will take. Don't hesitate to ask any questions before you leave and make sure you understand the chart.

have travelled even if the log is unreliable.

THE COURSE

First decide a route. Your choice will be influenced by how quickly you want to get there, whether you plan any stops on the way, if there are any dangers to avoid such as reefs or shoal patches, and whether the wind direction is favourable for sailing. A slightly longer route can be infinitely preferable to one where the wind is against you.

Plotting the course

To mark in your chosen route on the chart draw a series of straight lines using a pencil and the edge of a ruler or plotter. Keep it in mind that the lines will need to be erased later, so try not to be too heavy handed.

Some areas lend themselves quite well to directions such as 'Out of the harbour, turn left, and take the next turning right', but as direction at sea and distances from land can be misleading, and landmarks on shore are not always that easy to identify, it is necessary to have a more accurate way of determining direction.

THE COMPASS

This is where the compass comes in. A needle inside the compass points in the direction of the earth's magnetic north pole, and thereby tells you where south, east and west are as well as all the other points

in between. The position of magnetic north is not static, and is different from the earth's geographical or true north pole. This difference can be seen by looking at a compass rose on a chart. The outer ring gives directions related to true north, those on which the chart is based, while the inner offset ring gives directions related to magnetic north, which the compass will show. The difference between the two is known as variation. A compass reading taken on a boat will need to be converted to a true one in order for it to be applied to the chart, and vice versa.

Variation differs depending on where you are, so look at the rose nearest your position. In the centre you will find the variation given as degrees and minutes east or west for a particular year, and expected changes in subsequent years. A variation of 6' 12" (1991) decreasing 8" annually in three years will be 5 48W.

The simple ditty *'Variation West, Compass Best; Variation East, Compass Least'* helps many to remember how to apply variation in practice. If variation is west, then the compass reading will always be greater that on the chart, and if east, always less. If maths is not a strongpoint, remember that over small distances a mistake of a few degrees here and there will not be the end of the world, if you allow for errors and the fact that some people are better at steering a compass course than others. Most of us find it difficult to steer exactly to a course, and round it up or down to the nearest easy figure.

Your sailing area will probably be small enough to allow you to calculate the variation at the start of the holiday, and use the same figure throughout. If variation is approximately 5" West for example, just remember to add five degrees to any course taken from a chart when giving a course to steer, and take away five degrees from any compass course when applying it to the chart.

Deviation

If at any time you find your compass leading you off course, check you haven't left the pliers, flares or ghetto blaster (the speakers do it) anywhere nearby.

Compasses are affected by any magnetic influences, and are normally situated as far as possible from anything likely to cause what is known as deviation. This will be more pronounced on some courses than others, and those particularly affected such as steel ships carry a card showing how much deviation to the compass reading will occur on any particular heading. Fibreglass yachts have a smaller effect, though metal objects such as the engine can still cause problems. A compass course that has had no allowance made for deviation is officially known as a magnetic course. In practice few yachts carry deviation cards, which are not applicable to most leisure sailing.

COURSE TO STEER

To work out a course to steer, draw your first line from where you are (or just outside the harbour or bay) to the point at which you will need to change direction. Lay the edge of your plotter along this line. If you're using parallel rules, walk them across the chart until one edge runs through the exact centre of a compass rose, and read off the direction on the outer ring. If you have a Breton plotter, rotate the moveable wheel until its lines are in line with the grids on the chart and north is pointing to true north. Read off the direction on the wheel at the point indicated in the middle of the plotter. This is your true course.

Next apply variation. If there is no tide or current, and you are unlikely to be pushed off course by the wind, this is now your compass course to steer by. Make a note of it, and how far you must travel before reaching your destination. Work out courses to steer and distances to travel for the rest of the planned route.

POSITION

However good your planning, inevitably you will need to make allowances for events on the way such as an unfavourable wind direction or mutiny of the crew when it comes to lunchtime. You will need to know how to estimate your position at any point of the journey, and how to mark down your progress on the chart as you go along.

Leeway

You will need to estimate your leeway (the sideways movement away from the wind) when calculating how well you have managed to maintain the course you intended. To estimate how much leeway your yacht is making, turn around and look at the wake behind you. With a following wind the wake will be directly behind. With leeway, it will be deflected to one side, as the boat drifts sideways. Take a bearing of the wake with the hand bearing compass, and then another directly behind you. If the difference is five degrees, you are making five degrees of leeway. To calculate your new course, turn a little upwind and note which way the compass turns, and add or subtract five degrees from your original course accordingly. You may be unable to sail any closer to the wind, so take into account the effect of leeway when calculating where your course is taking you. Drawing an arrow on the chart to indicate wind direction can help you to visualise the effect the wind is having.

Dead reckoning

There are various ways of estimating your position when en route. Let's say that in a half hour period you know you have steered a particular course, noted a particular distance on the log, and estimated the leeway. Now apply variation and draw a line on the chart from where you started with a cross at the end to show how far along it you have travelled. You have now made a dead reckoning of your position.

If you then make allowances for any tidal streams pushing you off course or increasing or decreasing your speed, you can mark where you estimate yourself to be with a triangle, and this is known as your estimated position. Always mark down the time on the chart as well.

Taking a fix

Landmarks that are easily identifiable both physically and on the chart can be used to give you a more accurate idea of your position, by using them to take a fix. A three point fix is obtained by taking compass bearings of three separate landmarks and plotting them on the chart as position lines. Where they intersect is probably where you are.

You can bet that a big motor yacht like this has an impressive array of electronic wizardry - and a professional crew who know how to use it when following a complex route to the next anchorage.

To take a bearing, wear the hand-bearing compass around your neck and hold it up in the direction of an identified landmark. Allow it time to swing round into position and read off the bearing on the scale. Take all three bearings as quickly as possible so that you will not have changed position too much throughout the procedure. It may help to call out the readings to someone else to write down.

To plot a bearing as a position line on the chart, first convert it to a true bearing. If you have parallel rules, place an edge on the compass rose to intersect both the centre and the chosen bearing. Walk them over to the point on the chart on which you took the bearing, and draw a line from there to somewhere near where you think you are, and mark an arrow on the end nearest you. To use the Breton plotter, turn the wheel until the bearing lines up with the yacht's heading symbol, place an edge on the landmark, and turn the whole plotter until the wheel's *north* lines up with that on the chart, after which you draw a line

as before.

Plot all three position lines and see how they intersect. If they cross over exactly in the same spot, you probably have a fairly accurate fix. If they form a triangle in the middle (known as a cocked hat) you cannot be so certain of your position. Draw a circle where they intersect, and the time the bearings were taken. Rub out the rest of the lines to save cluttering up the chart. Sometimes it is only possible to take two bearings in which case your fix may be a little less reliable. Even if you can only get one bearing it can be useful in helping to determine where you are.

Some landmarks are more suitable than others. Buoys, for example, can shift position, and headlands look different depending on where you are viewing them from. Two landmarks close together can also be misleading, and ideally if two are used the angle between them should be around 90 degrees. If three are used, the angle between any two should be around 60 degrees. In practice you need to make the

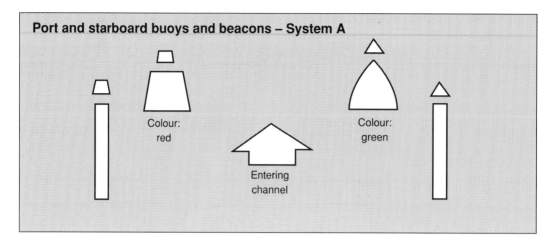

Port and starboard buoys and beacons – System A

best of what you have, but try to make sure you always have at least a fairly good idea as to where you are.

ELECTRONIC AIDS

Electronic aids such as Decca, Loran and the newer GPS systems are designed to pinpoint your position and can be extremely useful tools if their operation and limitations are fully understood. GPS systems have all manner of functions helping to make navigation easier, the simplest of which is giving a position in terms of latitude and longitude anywhere in the world.

PILOTAGE

Pilotage is about finding your way successfully in and out of harbours and confined areas such as narrow channels. The Pilot Guide, as its name suggests, is a vital source of information on what you can expect to find on entering a strange port, especially as few charts include such details.

Buoys and harbours

Harbours and approaches frequented by commercial vessels such as cargo ships usually have buoying systems to display deep water channels and mark hazards to navigation such as wrecks. Many harbours use leading lights or marks to guide boats in. In many holiday cruising grounds buoyed channels into harbours are few and far between, and many have nothing more than a light on the end of a harbour wall. Pilotage then consists of identifying conspicuous buildings or land features as highlighted by the pilot guide. Some areas use buoys to indicate reefs and dangers to smaller vessels, some (such as Greece) do not. Reefs and shoals in the Virgin Islands, for

example, are said to be well marked, but much less so in the Windwards and Leewards so it is wise to find out beforehand how much confidence may be placed in buoyage in any particular area.

The IALA system

IALA Maritime Buoyage is international, and throughout the world regions use either system A or B. System A is used throughout Europe, the Mediterranean, Australia, New Zealand and Thailand. System B is used throughout North, Central and South America, and the Caribbean (including the British Virgin Islands).

The IALA system identifies three types of buoy: lateral marks, cardinal marks, and some individual marks. In areas using system A, when entering a harbour buoys marking the left hand side of a channel are known as port hand marks, and are red and cylindrical. Any light will also be red. Those on the right are known as starboard hand marks and are green and conical, any light also being green. In system B, port hand marks are green and cylindrical, and starboard hand marks red and conical. Not all channels lead to harbours, and if there is likely to be any confusion the chart will show the symbol to indicate the direction of buoyage in use. If the direction of buoyage is being followed, port hand marks are left to port and starboard marks to starboard.

Cardinal marks are used to identify which side of a danger it is safe to pass. They are black and yellow pillar shaped buoys with distinctive top marks. Individual marks that exist as part of the IALA system are:
i)   Isolated danger marks placed on the danger itself.
ii)   Safe water marks to indicate safe water all around.

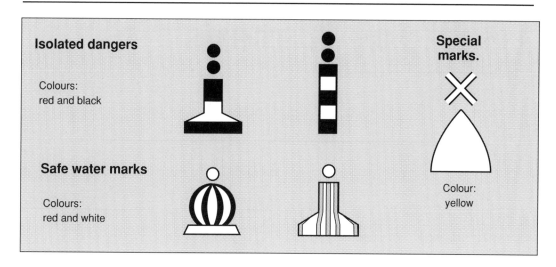

iii) Special marks – colour yellow, non-navigational for uses such as racing.

REEF NAVIGATION

When sailing in areas where reefs must be negotiated when entering a harbour or anchorage, many companies ask clients to be in by 4pm. This is because reefs are much easier to identify with the sun overhead, and extremely difficult with the sun in your eyes. Changes in water colour are a good guide. Deep water is generally an inky blue. Shallower water becomes lighter green, and when under 10 feet (3 metres) deep will become very light green if the bottom is sand. Rocks or coral will be light brown. It is a good idea to send someone to the bow to watch.

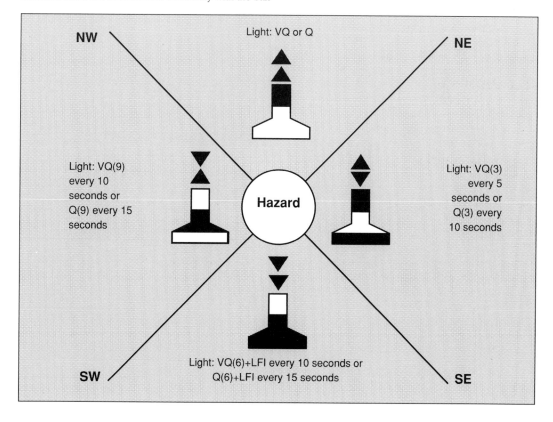

18 Tidal Waters

Some parts of the world are more tidal than others. In the Virgin Islands for example, tides are minimal depending on the time of year, whereas in Thailand tidal heights will be around three metres (10 feet). You need a bit more knowledge and experience to sail in tidal waters.

What causes tides?

Tides occur because the moon, and to a lesser extent the sun, exert a gravitational pull on the water covering the earth. The 'lumps' this causes (one lump on the moon side, and one on the opposite side of the earth) are high tide areas. As the earth spins these 'lumps' appear to move around its surface, giving most places two high tides and two low tides each day. Spring tides occur when the sun and moon are in line, giving their greatest effect. Neaps arise when the sun and moon are at right angles.

The tide ebbs (goes out) as the waterline recedes. It floods (comes in) as the waterline moves up the beach. Tidal streams are the currents created as large volumes move about. They are usually strongest midway between high and low tide.

Not all currents are tide induced. Other factors such as sea temperature differentials will cause currents that may be predominantly in one direction and peculiar to one part of the world, such as the north equatorial current that runs WNW through the Caribbean sea.

Although currents in the Mediterranean are rarely worth worrying about when it comes to navigation, apart from places like the Straits of Gibraltar and Messina, they do exist due to the fact that water there is evaporating faster than it can be replaced by rivers. This causes a continuous in-flow of surface water from the Atlantic Ocean which continues eastward and eventually sets up anti-clockwise currents in the western Mediterranean and in the Aegean and Adriatic seas, and a westerly flow along the northern shores of the Mediterranean in the east.

The Mediterranean is virtually non-tidal, with the exception of the far west area near the Straits of Gibraltar and narrow channels such as the Straits of Messina. Other parts of the world can have huge tidal ranges.

Land influences

Land masses influence the effect of currents. If water is made to flow over shallows, as around a headland, or is funnelled into a channel between islands, it will be made to travel faster and the current is therefore stronger. Even if a current flows in one direction, it may be deflected by any land it encounters such as an island. For these reasons, currents may be significant even when tidal height differences are not.

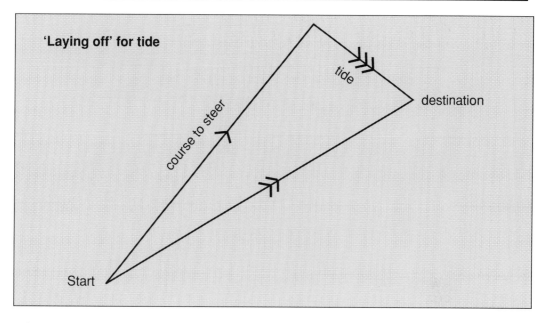

'Laying off' for tide

course to steer

tide

destination

Start

Tidal data

Tidal height differences and currents affect sailing in two ways. Firstly they effect navigation. Not only do you need to know how much water there is beneath you, such as when negotiating your way into an anchorage, but you also need to be able to calculate the effect any current is having on your progress on the way. Secondly, boat handling can be made much more difficult by a current especially when you are manoeuvring in a confined space and if it is strong.

Tidal data can be presented as tide tables, tidal stream atlases and on charts, and relevant data should be part of the navigational equipment on board when chartering. Information concerning any other currents affecting the area is often to be found in a pilot guide. Tidal data is not easily interpreted, one of the reasons being that it is often necessary to work out data for one place or time from that given for another, a process commonly known as interpolation. When sailing around coastlines strongly influenced by tides these calculations are important, though how many people actually work things out to the last decimal point is another matter. If the tidal range is only slight, minute calculations of depth will not be appropriate.

Tidal stream effects

When working out your position you will need to know the effect the tidal stream is having, especially if you do not have convenient landmarks for bearings. Tidal atlases show this fairly simply with arrows showing the rate and direction of flow at any particular time and place. Charts may use a symbol such as a diamond to mark points on the chart, with a table to refer to for information about rate and direction of flow at that point. These are usually marked in places where effects are significant.

In British Admiralty atlases and charts, times are in relation to the time of high water in a port such as Dover. Two figures show the difference in rates depending on whether you are at springs or neaps or somewhere between the two. On charts, direction of stream is given as a true bearing. Spring tides occur around the time of a full or new moon when gravitational effects are stronger, and neaps at around the half moon when they are weaker. The difference between low and high water levels known as the tidal range is greater with a spring tide, and tidal streams are stronger as well.

To find out what allowances to make for tidal stream when working out a course to steer, draw a line between where you are and your destination. Find out the direction of the tidal stream and draw a line in that direction from your starting point. To mark off how far the stream will move in that direction over a period of one hour, find out the rate, and use the dividers to measure it from the latitude scale. Transfer the dividers to the line depicting the direction of tidal stream and mark off the distance. If you were simply to try and stay put at the starting point, this is where the tide would have taken you after one hour.

Estimate how fast you think you will be able to go over a period of one hour and use the dividers to

Will we dry out? Marinas in tidal areas solve the problem by using floating pontoons which go up and down with the tide, or in some cases the water in the marina is held at a constant height by a lock.

measure it. Place one end of the dividers on the point marked off on the end of the tidal stream direction line, and swing the other end round until it crosses the original line drawn to where you want to go. Mark off this point and draw a line between the two. This is the direction you will need to steer to counter the effect of the stream, and end up where you wanted to be. Do not forget to convert it to a compass bearing, and allow for leeway.

The technique can also be used to work out the tidal effect retrospectively and therefore where you will be, having followed a particular course. In this case the tidal stream line is drawn at the end of your course line.

WILL WE DRY OUT?

When deciding where to anchor in a bay, you need to know that you will not go aground at low water, and how much anchor line to let out to hold you at all states of the tide.

If there were no tide, you would know to allow yourself a certain minimum below the waterline. Let's suppose the yacht draws 1.8 metres (6 feet) for example, at which point the echo sounder will read only 1.3 metres as it is 0.5 metres below the waterline.

You may decide the minimum depth is three metres (10 feet), or 2.5 metres on the echo sounder.

Tidal heights for a particular place are usually given for high and low water along with the times they occur. If the height of tide at the next low water is 1.3 metres for example, and you are able to calculate that the height of tide at the moment is 3.5 metres, then you know that at the next low water the level is going to have dropped to 2.2 metres compared with what you've got now, even if at the moment it is on its way up to high water. If you want three metres below your waterline at low water, you will need to anchor in at least 5.2 metres.

Rule of twelfths

Calculating the height of tide where you are may not be straightforward. You may need to work from a tidal curve diagram, or interpolate data from somewhere else. However, it is often possible to gain a rough idea by using what is known as the rule of twelfths.

This is a means of approximating how far the water level has risen or fallen at a particular point in the tidal cycle (though some places are subject to local variations in which case it may be unreliable).

The rule of twelfths is that the tide will rise or fall

by 1/12 in the first and 6th hours; by 2/12 in the second and 5th; and by 3/12 in the third and fourth. If the tidal range (difference between low and high water) is 3.6 metres for example, one twelfth of that is 0.3 metres:

1st	1/12	0.3	0.3
2nd	2/12	0.6	0.9
3rd	3/12	0.9	1.8
4th	3/12	0.9	2.7
5th	2/12	0.6	3.3
6th	1/12	0.3	3.6

If high water for example was at 9.00, and the time is now 12.00, it is the end of the third hour, and the level will have dropped approximately 1.8 metres below what it was at high water, with another 1.8 metres to go until low water. To keep three metres below your waterline, you would need to anchor in 4.8 metres. If the water was on its way up as opposed to down, and you know the present low water to be 1.2 metres, the present height of the tide is therefore 3 metres (1.2 + 1.8). If the next low water is only 0.9 metres, then you know that the water will fall 2.1 metres from where it is now, and you would need to anchor in 5.1 metres to still have 3 metres beneath you at the next low water.

Do not forget to allow for the yacht swinging towards the shore when the tide starts to come back in. This may put you in shallower water. A chart will not give specific depths close in to shore which is why you have to work them out in this way.

How much line?

When calculating how much line to lay, you will need to know the depth of water you will be in at the next high tide, and use sufficient scope accordingly. If the height of tide at low water is 1.2 metres and at high water 6.1 metres, then the range is 5.9 metres. Add this to the depth you have calculated to be in at low water, and you will have the maximum depth.

If you have to tie up alongside a wall, be careful to have the mooring lines slack enough to allow the yacht to move up and down as required. Long bow and stern lines are better than breast lines, and it is advisable to have someone remain on board.

19 Using A VHF Radio

Even a craft as grand as this will be equipped with a VHF radio, and may be listening out for you.

You may find you use your VHF (very high frequency) radio far more than you have been used to. Many countries require an operator's licence, but in others such as Greece a VHF licence for the boat is all that is required and it should be found in your boat papers.

Use of marine VHF radio is strictly controlled around countries such as Britain, but not so much in others where at times it seems as if channels are being used as an alternative to the telephone. Remember that a VHF radio can be a lifeline for a boat in trouble, so keep the emergency channel (channel 16 throughout the world) clear for anything but initial calling and distress calls. Be aware that other callers may be trying to use your chosen channel as well, and keep calls to a sensible minimum.

Many charter companies, and particularly flotillas, use a pre-determined channel on which to listen and call up other boats and shore staff. This will be one that is not normally in use for anything else, and avoids the use of channel 16. Keeping a listening watch on this particular channel means you can be informed of any changes in itinerary or expected bad weather. You will also hear if anyone in the area requires assistance, as many boats may be using the same channel. Some radios have a facility for listening to channel 16 at the same time (dual watch). If you need urgent assistance yourself that warrants a mayday call, use channel 16, and if you know there is help in the area such as the flotilla support crew, put out a call on their channel as well.

Operation of a VHF radio is comparatively easy. Don't be embarrassed about using one, but don't hog the airwaves.

For longer conversations, call up on the pre-determined channel, and then switch to another. Check at your boat briefing which channels to use.

How to use the VHF radio

However sophisticated the design, knowledge of a few basic controls will be enough to enable you to use a VHF radio. Some countries such as Britain demand that at least one person on board holds an operator's licence.

1. Switch on the power supply. There may be a switch on the instrument control panel as well as on the radio itself. Often the volume control is incorporated in the on/off switch. The volume will need to be set higher if you are in the cockpit or have the engine running. Sometimes there will be an external speaker in the cockpit which can be turned on or off as required.

2. The squelch control allows you to cut out the noise that accompanies VHF signals. Start by turning the squelch control to the lowest position, and slowly turn it up until the noise stops. If the squelch is turned too high you will not receive all signals, so keep it on the borderline. It may need readjusting from time to time.

3. VHF radios can be operated on either low or high power (1 watt and 25 watts respectively). Low power is sufficient for short range calls such as when entering a harbour, and restricts the area in which you transmit as well as receive. High power allows communication over a greater area, but as VHF signals travel in straight lines and do not follow the curvature of the earth, their range is limited by the height of the aerial and any land masses that are in the way. VHF aerials are normally situated at the highest point possible, at the top of the mast. Emergency calls should always be transmitted on high power.

4. Turn the radio to the desired channel by means of the dial or push-button controls. Newer radios will have a digital display. If you want to transmit, make sure to turn off any dual watch facility.

5. VHF radios are not able to receive and transmit at

the same time. To transmit a message, take the microphone in one hand, depress the transmit button on the side and speak into it clearly. When you have finished, say the word "Over" and release the button.

Whoever you are calling will now know they can reply. Listen for them to say "Over" before trying to speak again because no signal will get through while they are still transmitting. Do not get too worried about what you sound like or if you are saying all the right things. If it makes you nervous, think beforehand what you want to say, and if it helps, write it down.

What to say

To call another yacht, speak their yacht name twice, followed by your yacht name twice, and finish with "Over". For example, "Nafsika, Nafsika, this is Melody, Melody, over". They should reply with "Melody, this is Nafsika over". You are now free to continue the conversation. End your final transmission with "Out" to signal you have finished. "Over and out" contains two conflicting messages, so just "Out" will do.

If you have no pre-determined channel, you will need to make your initial call on channel 16, and move to another as quickly as possible to keep it clear. Your call should go as follows: "Nafsika, Nafsika, this is Melody, Melody, channel 6, over". The reply should be: "Melody, this is Nafsika, channel 6,over". Confirm you have heard them by repeating "Nafsika, Melody, Channel 6, over", then switch to channel 6 and wait for their reply. Any change of channels can be done this way.

Sometimes you will make a call and receive no answer. You may not have been heard, either because you were too far away or because there were stronger signals being transmitted in the area at the same time. Alternatively, you may have been heard but for some reason are not able to hear the reply. Check the squelch control, and then leave it a few minutes before trying again to avoid blocking the channel and irritating other users by repeating the same call over and over again. Even though the channel sounds clear, there may be others using it that you are not aware of.

English is the international language for use on radio, but in practice you will hear many others being broadcast as well. It took us a while to realise that the yacht "Cambio" was in fact no such thing, but simply Italian for "Over"! Many countries broadcast weather reports, usually in English. Ask on which channels and at what times.

Mayday!

The word 'Mayday' is internationally recognised as a distress call, and should be used if there is grave danger to vessel or to the life of a person or persons on board, that requires immediate assistance, such as if the boat is sinking or about to sink, or you have a man overboard who you are not able to retrieve.

A call using the words 'Pan Pan' as opposed to 'Mayday' indicates a very urgent or potentially grave situation concerning the safety of vessel or a person, such as if someone needs urgent medical attention. Both are a general broadcast to anyone in the area, be it coastguard, ship or another yacht.

Mayday procedure

First make sure the radio is switched on, turned to high power, and tuned to channel 16. Do not wait for a reply before completing the whole message. Speak slowly and clearly for anyone whose first language is not English.

1. "Mayday" spoken three times.
2. "Yacht Name" spoken three times.
3. "Mayday".
4. "Yacht Name".
5. "My position is....."

Give your position as distance and bearing from a point on land, for example "One mile, zero four five degrees from Cap Corse", or if you have it, your latitude and longitude. If you only know approximately where you are, be sure to make that clear.

6. Nature of the distress – "On fire".
7. Assistance required – "Request immediate assistance".
8. Other information – "Sailing yacht, four persons on board".
9. End your call with "Over" (and remember to take your finger off the transmit button). Allow time for a reply. If no one does, repeat the call at intervals. Repeat the whole message because someone may be able to hear you, but not be able to get through.

20 Problems and Emergencies

On a flotilla it is reassuring to be able to call up the support crew, and get them to come to your aid quickly.

This chapter deals with some of the things that can go wrong. Some you will be able to fix, some will need outside help. Knowing what to do in each case can make a huge difference to the effect the problem has on your holiday.

Support crews

One of the reasons people choose a flotilla holiday is that they will be able to call on the services of the flotilla support crew should they need to. Support crews are often very used to dealing with a problem that you may be encountering for the first time, and you can call for advice at any time. Bareboat charterers also usually have access to support.

Some companies operate both bareboat and flotilla charters in the same area and recommend that bareboat people contact flotilla staff if advice or help is required. Many bareboat charter companies provide back-up services, such as a mobile engineer, and will advise how and when to call for assistance.

Other help

As well as knowing how to call company services, find out beforehand how to call regular services such as the coastguard. In some areas such as the British Virgin Islands, coast radio stations can put you in touch with a doctor or hospital in the event of your needing medical help. Keep a note of appropriate VHF

When you are motoring for long distances, make regular checks on the engine. Sadly there's a lot of debris floating in the sea, and it's possible you may suck up a plastic bag.

channels and phone numbers where they are easy to find in a hurry. Although the amount of assistance available to yachts varies from place to place, channel 16 is always available for Mayday and Pan Pan calls in the event of serious or life-threatening situations. Ships listen out on channel 16 as well, and may have other services to hand such as a doctor.

If a company is unable to send someone out to deal with a problem, they may suggest you call on a local service such as an engineer. It helps to know beforehand who they recommend, and checking with the company first can make it easier when it comes to sorting out any bills. You may of course have no choice but to seek assistance from whoever you can find if the need is urgent.

Even if the problem is non-urgent, and you are able to cope at present, it is advisable to inform those concerned such as the flotilla support crew, so that they can either come out and see you, or listen out for

you and come to your assistance as required.

Sometimes you may be offered assistance from another boat. They may do so expecting nothing in return, but be aware that under salvage laws a boat giving assistance to another (such as a tow) may be entitled to claim a substantial sum of money for the service, so you should try and find out beforehand if they intend to charge you, and if so agree a price. Understandably this may be the last thing that concerns you at the time, but it could come as a shock later on. Marine insurance covers such claims, but if you were found to be at fault you could stand to lose your security deposit.

In the event of situations requiring urgent assistance, do not delay in seeking professional help, even if another yacht is offering help as well.

ENGINE PROBLEMS

If an engine fault light shows, a buzzer sounds or a gauge indicates a fault, turn off the engine. Only use the engine in an emergency. If the problem cannot be resolved, and you are unable to sail to where you need to go, you will need to seek assistance.

Insufficient oil pressure

First check the oil level (never with the engine running!). If there is no oil or the level is below the minimum, either the engine has used it up or it has leaked out. If a leak is not immediately obvious, top up the oil. A major oil leak into the engine compartment will be very obvious, but it will probably be difficult to tell where it has come from with so much oil about. Clean up with plenty of washing-up liquid and water, and check to see if the dipstick is still in place. If possible, refill between minimum and maximum and try and identify the leak. Look for any burst pipes or leaking seals. An engine that is run without oil will seize, stop and not restart, and will either need a total replacement or major repairs.

Overheating

Check to see if there is any cooling water coming from the exhaust. If there is none or only a small amount and steam, stop the engine. (It would be very unlikely for overheating to occur with normal amounts of cooling water.) A small amount plus perhaps steam can mean a restricted water intake, and no cooling water can mean a blocked intake, or less likely a problem with the water pump. Continuing to use the engine will cause damage to the water pump (if that itself is not the cause), followed by damage to the engine.

Mediterranean harbours are frequently full of small moorings. Don't attempt to go in amongst a mass of lines.

1. Is the seacock on the intake fully on? It could have been partly turned off by mistake when stowing something nearby.

2. Is the filter blocked?

3. Is there something such as seaweed or a plastic bag blocking the intake from the outside? If the water is warm and calm and you feel like a swim, jump in and check. Otherwise try getting into the dinghy and feeling underneath with your hand.

If it is none of these, there could be a blockage further up the pipe, or there could be a problem with the pump itself (such as jamming with debris) or even a broken shaft. Always check the simple explanations first before trying anything more complex. It may of course be possible to sail to where you want to go, by which time the engine should have cooled down enough to allow you to use it.

FOULED PROPELLER

Having something wrap around your propeller can cause serious problems, and is best avoided. To help, we've listed the most common causes.

1. Lines beneath you such as anchor lines, fixed mooring lines and mooring buoys.

2. Lines from the boat such as genoa sheets, furling lines, mooring lines and the dinghy painter.

3. Floating debris such as plastic bags, pieces of old line and seaweed.

4. Fishing nets and tackle

Fishing lines

Fishing practices vary from place to place, and it is a good idea to know what to look out for in your particular area. Mediterranean fishermen frequently use nets that sink below the surface but are buoyed at both ends. Buoys may simply be pieces of polystyrene, perhaps with a black plastic bin liner flag. Some floating nets are used and although they should be out of the way of most boats, you might come across them in bays or close to shore. Lobster pots will have a buoy attached, and in parts of the Caribbean fish traps may be marked by two buoys joined together so that the second floats downwind of the first, making it important not to pass between them.

Harbours

Be careful in harbours or anchorages where laid moorings are used, or where people are mooring bows-to or stern-to a quay. Chain lines normally sink and are therefore less likely to be a problem, but mooring buoys are frequently attached with floating lines. It's safer to pull your boat out from a mooring with the anchor line rather than driving out. Only engage gear when you're clear of all lines and have tidied your own anchor line. You can help prevent another boat fouling its propeller on your anchor line by letting off the tension and allowing it to sink if they come too near, but make sure there is some other means of stopping your boat hitting the quay while you do so.

Level of damage

Damage, if any, will depend on what is wrapped around the propeller, and how tightly. Weed will normally be severed by the rotating blades, but a tightly wrapped line can cause major damage. Initially there will be a decrease in engine revs, sometimes accompanied by black smoke from the exhaust as the engine labours under the increased load. Next the boat will slow down, and if the obstruction does not clear, the engine will eventually stop if allowed to keep running in gear. The faster the engine revs, the longer it will take for the obstruction to stop it, and the more damage will be done.

As a line wraps around the propeller and rotating shaft, it may be forced between the propeller and shaft support, the *P-bracket*. This will pull the shaft, and may damage the stern gland, gearbox, or engine mountings. If the line is fixed at one end, it will tighten as the propeller turns, and bend the propeller shaft and P-bracket. A serious bend in the P-bracket will allow the propeller to hit the bottom of the boat, with serious consequences.

Pre-emptive action

It is usually possible to stop such a situation before it ever gets that far. If, for example, you find yourself drifting over another anchor line when coming into a mooring, keep the engine in neutral and push the line underneath your rudder with the boathook. A loosely wrapped line will cause no damage as long as the propeller is stopped from turning.

An unexpected decrease in engine revs can be alarming. If it happens, put the engine into neutral which should make the revs pick up again. Check over the side for obvious causes such as a line over the side. If it is tight this may be easy to miss. A piece of weed or a plastic bag may clear spontaneously, or by putting the engine into neutral and then into forwards or reverse, but you still need to be sure of the cause before attempting to use the engine. What you do next will depend on where you are. If you are

entering a harbour or anchorage, the priority will be to make the boat safe before anything else, such as by dropping an anchor or tying up to another yacht if you are that close. If you are out at sea, you may be able to drift about and find out what is wrong, or sail to where it is safer and easier to do so.

Freeing the prop

If a line such as a genoa sheet is only loosely wrapped, it may be possible to free it by pulling gently on it while turning the propeller shaft from inside the boat (and with the engine off!). This will only be successful with loose wraps. If the line is tight, there will usually be a riding turn or turns, and pulling on them may only make them tighter.

When trying to undo a wrap from underneath the boat, any tension on the line will make it impossible. If you are fixed to someone's anchor line, you will need to ask for their co-operation in giving you some slack. You may need to drop an anchor yourself if held on a fixed line, to take off any tension on the one you are trying to undo. If you are able to remain below the water for a reasonable length of time, you could try wrapping the free end of line around the propeller blades and turning the propeller to try and pull the coils apart, but always be careful of getting entangled in any lines when underneath the boat.

Cutting free

Sometimes the line will be so jammed there will be no option but to cut it free, in which case it is important to make sure that all the line is removed. Cutting a fishing net or someone else's mooring should be avoided if at all possible. Someone may prefer you to ask for their assistance rather than hack at their line from a dinghy! If you do need to cut it, make sure not to loose anything that was on the other end such as an anchor or lobster pot.

Once the propeller is cleared, check for damage. Check the P-bracket when you are down there. Check for water coming into the boat, from the stern gland. Have a look to see if the shaft has moved or if the engine mountings are bent. Noisy vibration with the engine in gear indicates that something is out of alignment, due to a bent shaft or damaged gearbox or mountings, and must be looked at professionally as soon as possible. It is advisable to contact your charter company as soon as you can to check if any action should be taken in the event of a tightly wrapped propeller. If you are unable to clear the propeller fully, you will need to seek assistance anyway.

Unless you drive a yacht hard on the bottom, it should be easy enough to get it off again. In some cruising areas it is very deep close in to the shore and you can approach with no problem.

GOING AGROUND

The most important thing about going aground is to avoid it in the first place. Don't cut corners when entering a bay, check the chart for depths and dangers, avoid shallows, approach the shore slowly, and avoid taking risks. The faster you go aground, the harder getting off is likely to be. Be careful of being blown onto a lee shore, and if you are in tidal waters know whether the tide is going up or down, and in which direction it is trying to take you. If you are unsure of tidal heights, be on the safe side and go by chart datum. Just because there was enough water to put you on the ground, it does not mean there will be

enough to lift you off when the tide comes back in. Generally, be extra careful when the tide is ebbing (going out) because if you go aground you could be there until the next tide.

Heel the boat

If you find yourself aground, and there is no rising tide to lift you off, reduce the draft of the boat heeling her and use the engine or sails to drive it off. No time should be lost if the tide is on its way down. A yacht can be made to heel by moving weight such as the crew onto one side. Hang onto the boom as it is extended out over the side to increase the effect,

This is just what you don't want to pick up on your anchor, particularly if it's a chain or heavy wire cable. If it's a line, try to lift it off using a loop of rope.

though be careful of falling in. Often the sails will do just as well, but may also contribute to pushing you further onto a lee shore. If this is happening, take them down.

Pull the boat off

If none of this works, you can try using an anchor to drag yourself off. Take it out in the dinghy with as long a line as possible and drop it as far away from the boat as you can. It is probably best to try and get off in the same direction as that you got on from, though a boathook can help tell you which way seems deepest. Keep the yacht heeled, use the engine, and pull on the anchor line. Be careful not to allow any slack to dangle in the water near the stern of the boat and risk wrapping the prop.

Going aground can fall anywhere between two extremes. On the one hand it is calm, there is no onshore wind to worry about, you are resting on mud and there is no falling tide to rush for. On the other it is rough, you are on a lee shore and being pushed onto rocks. The first should be fairly easy to deal with, but the second will probably need assistance.

Towing skills

Towing demands good boat handling skill, and can be dangerous in shallow water, windy conditions and when the crew panic. So it is not always advisable to seek assistance from another yacht, or to offer it yourself. If hull damage has occurred, pulling the yacht off could cause it to take in water, so professional help is required. If someone does offer you a line, be careful to secure it well and prevent it dangling in the water near your stern. Make sure the

crew are safe, and be ready to steer and motor away as soon as you become free so as to avoid any collision. An assisting yacht may have a deeper draft and must be very careful not to go aground herself. Always try to find out if an assisting vessel intends to charge for a tow. Check for any damage afterwards, especially after being on rocky ground.

FOULED ANCHORS

Crossed anchor lines can cause problems for two reasons. Firstly, the holding of the anchor underneath may be compromised. For instance, if the wind blows up one anchor may drag and take the other with it. Secondly, an anchor can be extremely difficult to lift if there is any weight of line lying across it. If there is chain lying across it, lifting is likely to be exceptionally difficult, and an old, barnacle-encrusted chain may also damage the boat.

Careful mooring

Being sure you have not crossed another line or had your own crossed when anchoring in a bay may not be possible, and changes in wind and tide will require you to keep an eye on your position, in relation to other boats as well as to the shore. Other skippers may help by pointing out where their anchor lies as you approach, and sometimes it is possible to get a better idea of the situation once you are anchored by taking a swim with a mask and snorkel, though weed can make it difficult to see where lines lie.

Theoretically it is easier to avoid crossed lines when mooring to a quay, but it is not always easy to get it right. Try not to make it difficult for others to avoid your line, by not laying your anchor at too great an angle to the quay.

Leave alone?

If lines are crossed but both anchors appear to be holding well, the decision may be to leave the situation alone, especially if mooring was difficult. If you have crossed another line, the other boat may be justified in asking you to move it, because it takes away their ability to move from the quay quickly should they need to. If you do not want to leave the quay, you could lay a second anchor with the dinghy, and then take up the first. If the other boat decides it is OK to leave it be, make sure you know what time they wish to leave, and if necessary be prepared to leave first.

You may not always be sure if lines are crossed. Sometimes fouling only occurs as an anchor is raised, and is inadvertently dragged over another's line in the process of pulling it back onto the boat.

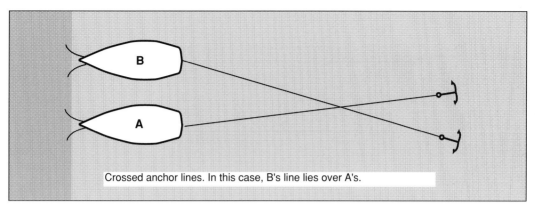

Crossed anchor lines. In this case, B's line lies over A's.

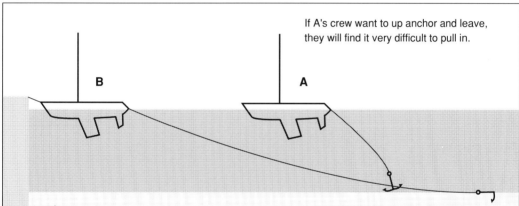

If A's crew want to up anchor and leave, they will find it very difficult to pull in.

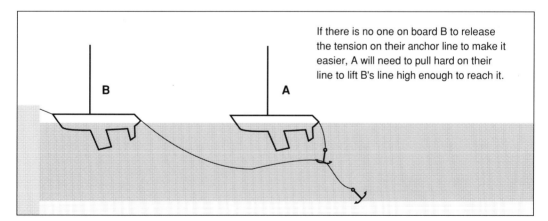

If there is no one on board B to release the tension on their anchor line to make it easier, A will need to pull hard on their line to lift B's line high enough to reach it.

Changing lines

If you know your line to be crossed, it may be possible to free it before leaving the quay by undoing the end of your line, and passing it under and back over the other one, so that now your line lies on top. If you find your line to be crossed as you try and pull up the anchor, you will need to keep pulling until the anchor is nearly up, and the line that is crossing your line is

pulled near enough to the surface to be able to take hold of. The anchor can then be freed from underneath.

If the line is difficult to lift, pass a length of line around it and hold it with that, making sure to cleat off both ends before taking the strain as the anchor is let go. If there is anyone on board the boat with the other anchor line, they can help you by letting the tension off

Remember that freeing your anchor from a crossed line may disturb the other anchor. Do not leave the boat it is attached to drifting.

You've blocked the toilet again!!! One advantage of a flotilla is that there's always a friendly and occasionally long- suffering support crew to sort it out for you.

their anchor line and making it easier to pull up.

Freeing an anchor from a crossed line will frequently disturb the other one as well, so if possible do not leave without making sure that someone has re-tensioned the anchor line on the other boat. If there was no one on board at the time, they could come back and find their boat hitting the quay. In the same way, if your line is stopping another yacht lifting their line, let off the line and give plenty of slack, making sure to hold the boat off the quay with someone on shore, or a spring line to the boat next door. If the crossing line is very heavy, and you can identify which boat it is attached to, take your anchor line out from underneath by undoing the end and uncrossing it from the dinghy, being careful not to let your yacht drift while the anchor is unattached.

If your line is caught beneath another line when at anchor, wind or tide may cause you to come together and possibly collide as you pull on your line and it slides up along their line. Fenders should prevent any damage.

Perils on the bottom

Sometimes an anchor can be difficult to lift and just needs a good pull with a winch to break it free. Sometimes they become caught on something, such as a rock, bits of old junk or heavy chain mooring line.

Check in the pilot if such chains are a hazard, and avoid anchoring near them. Fixed mooring lines in a marina are an indication not to drop an anchor. If a harbour is fairly shallow, a good swimmer may be able to swim down and free an anchor, or at least attach a trip line. If visibility is bad he can follow the anchor line down to the bottom. Others may be too

deep, in which case there is probably a diver around who is used to being asked to free anchors from mooring chains (for a fee of course).

If for any reason you do find your anchor fouled and seemingly impossible to lift, try lifting it as far as you can and then quickly dropping it before trying to lift it again. If you are lucky it may drop out from underneath whatever was holding it. Try altering the angle of attack by motoring in different directions, but be careful not to drive over the line and foul the propeller. A trip line is a precautionary measure against fouling the anchor, and you may be advised to use one in situations where there is a significant risk.

BLOCKED TOILETS & SINKS
The simple blockage

Marine toilets are less able to handle bulky waste such as paper than conventional toilets due to their relatively narrow piping and their pumping systems. Items such as tampons will most definitely be too much for the average system to cope with. You may be advised at the briefing not to put paper down the toilet, or perhaps only to use small amounts. It is probably true to say that the more paper used, the more blockages are likely to occur, especially where holding tanks are concerned, as paper tends to float to the top and remain inside, eventually building up and causing a blockage at the outflow pipe. If you are given the choice, you may consider the inconvenience of putting used paper into a bag – a small price to pay for a trouble free toilet.

Other causes and cures

A simple reason for a toilet not to work is trying to use

Trip Lines

If the sea bed is rocky, a trip line attached to the crown of the anchor will often allow it to be pulled up if the flukes are fouled. Either take the end of the line back to the yacht, or float a fender on it.

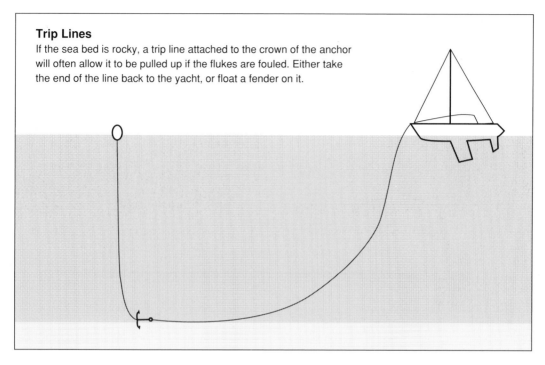

it with a seacock turned off. A stiff pump can often be freed by pouring a little vegetable oil into the bowl and pumping it through. (Don't use mineral oils such as engine oil.) Toilets that use suction to draw sea water in (Lavac) have a bleed hole in the inlet pipe, and this must be kept clear, so avoid hanging things over the top of it such as wet weather gear. Toilet blockages tend to occur at restrictions in the system such as at pump valves and pipe entries and exits.

A blockage at the bowl can often be cleared by persistent flushing. If the system uses a vacuum to draw flushing water in it will require a bucket of water to flush a blockage at this point. Water and toilet cleaner left to soak in the bowl may help to clear it if flushing does not work, as may a plunger if there is one on board.

A plastic bag or weed can cause a blockage at the seawater intake, so if there is no sign of blockage in the bowl this can be the next place to check. If the toilet is electrically operated, check the supply. Unfortunately all other problem areas are inaccessible without dismantling parts of the system, which as well as being a very unpleasant task can cause further problems with pipe and seacock connections. Don't detach anything without first making sure the seacocks are turned off. The best thing to do is seek assistance and in the meantime make do with shore toilets or a bucket.

Holding tanks

If your holding tank blocks, it will fill up. Thereafter, continuing to use the toilet will cause waste to exit via the breather pipe, though as this is fairly narrow it may soon become blocked as well. Be careful of inviting the wrath of harbour authorities and indeed other harbour users, and possibly incurring a very large fine.

Blocked sinks

Sinks are usually blocked by food waste or small items such as the top of a toothpaste tube. The pipe itself is fairly narrow and there is often no guard at the top.

There may be a plunger on board but if not try creating suction by using a cupped hand, palm down over the hole. A few swift pulls up and down may cure the problem, as may a finger pushed in and out a few times. A few pumps with a dinghy pump, with its end inserted into the hole can blow the blockage free, and you may even find the offending items floating in the sink if water is allowed to back-flow with the boat heeled to that side. If nothing else works, try inserting a piece of wire such as an unbent coat hanger, but be careful not to damage the pipe. Trying to remove a pipe from its connection is not recommended, as they are frequently held in place with a sealant as well as a pipe clip, and vigorous pulling can do damage, to the sink itself.

Other yachting titles from Fernhurst Books

Boat Cuisine *by June Raper*
Boat Engines 3e *by Dick Hewitt*
Bottoms Up *by Robert Watson*
Celestial Navigation *by Tom Cunliffe*
Children Afloat *by Pippa Driscoll*
Coastal & Offshore Navigation *by Tom Cunliffe*
Cruising Crew *by Malcolm McKeag*
Cruising Skipper *by John Mellor*
Electronics Afloat *by Tim Bartlett*
First Aid Afloat *by Dr. Robert Haworth*
Heavy Weather Cruising *by Tom Cunliffe*
Inshore Navigation *by Tom Cunliffe*
Knots & Splices *by Jeff Toghill*
Log Book for Cruising under Sail *by John Mellor*
Marine VHF Operation *by Michael Gale*
Ready About! *by Mike Peyton*
Sail to Freedom *by Bill & June Raper*
Sailing: A Beginner's Manual *by John Driscoll*
Simple Electronic Navigation *by Mik Chinery*
Simple GPS Navigation *by Mik Chinery*
Weather at Sea *by David Houghton*

If you would like a free full-colour brochure please write, phone or fax us:

Fernhurst Books,
Duke's Path, High Street, Arundel, West Sussex BN18 9AJ, England

Telephone: 01903 882277 Fax: 01903 882715